HOURS OF INVIGORATING WORDPLAY

The Literate Puzzler

Rita Norr Provost
Audrey Tumbarello

BARNES
& NOBLE

NEW YORK

ISBN-13: 978-0-7607-8917-9
ISBN-10: 0-7607-8917-7

Printed and bound in the United States of America

1 3 5 7 9 10 8 6 4 2

• Contents •

Acknowledgments

Thanks to our families for tolerating missed meals and frenzied schedules. To our agent, Elizabeth Knappman, our gratitude for continued confidence and support. Particular thanks to Ann Dietz for her expertise in puns and anagrams. Also, our appreciation to our friends in the Scrabble community, especially the Park Slope Scrabblettes and Ann Sanfedele. And to Jeanette Green, our editor at Sterling, thanks for diligent attention to detail, which gave us our "traveling shoes."

• **Word Structure** •

"X" Marks the Spot

Use the whimsical and punny definitions below to find these words which contain the letter "X" plunk in the middle.

1. Physical attribute of some women __ __ X __ __
2. A mister who repairs things F I X - I T
3. Lots of guts M O X I E
4. Louis or shorts __ __ X __ __
5. Called the Lone Star T E X A S
6. Tinkerbell, for one P I X I E
7. Chemically, two of O __ __ __ X __ __ __
8. Literary don Q U I X O T E
9. Not very clear __ __ __ X __ __ __
10. People acting in place of others __ __ __ X __ __ __
11. Some political leaders __ __ __ X __ __ __ or __ __ __ X __ __ __ __
12. Not exactly authoritative __ __ __ __ X __ __ __ __
13. Some blondes __ __ __ __ X __ __ __ __
14. Highly disagreeable __ __ __ __ X __ __ __ __
15. Phone-o-grams __ __ X __ __
16. Homely homily __ __ X __ __
17. Blender job __ __ X - __ __

Split Ends

Add one letter to the beginning and one letter to the end of these words to make another ordinary word. Do *not* use an "S" in the beginning or end.

Example: A̲ M U L E T̲

1. __ R E S T __
2. __ A X E S __
3. __ B O A R __
4. __ O T I C __
5. __ H O R A L __
6. __ U R E A __
7. __ A L E E __
8. __ A M E N __
9. __ P I N E __
10. __ O V E R T __
11. __ H O R N __
12. __ L O W E R __
13. __ P L A N __
14. __ R U G A __
15. __ I M I D E __

16. __ I L I A __
17. __ H E A P __
18. __ U N D E __
19. __ A B R I __
20. __ U N D O __
21. __ H I D __
22. __ R Y A __
23. __ M O N __
24. __ Y E N __
25. __ V A T __
26. __ U R B __
27. __ A C T __
28. __ B A T __
29. __ E L S __
30. __ F I R __

Split Ends II

Add one letter to the beginning and one letter to the end of these words to make another ordinary word. Do *not* use an "S" in the beginning or end.

Example: C L I N G Y

1. __ R E E D __

2. __ R A V E R __

3. __ I D E S __

4. __ E U R O __

5. __ W O K E __

6. __ Q U A T E __

7. __ W H I R __

8. __ E N O W __

9. __ H A N G __

10. __ O N U S __

11. __ I S B A __

12. __ R O Q U E __

13. __ V I L L __

14. __ I M P I __

15. __ R A T I O __

16. __ R A G I __

17. __ L E A S __

18. __ N O P E __

19. __ I N I A __

20. __ I N T E R __

21. __ P A R __

22. __ M O T __

23. __ E G G __

24. __ V I E __

25. __ I R K __

26. __ A D S __

27. __ P I S __

28. __ J I N __

29. __ O L D __

30. __ E L D __

Split Ends III

Add one letter to the beginning and one letter to the end of these words to make another ordinary word. Do *not* use an "S" in the beginning or end.

Example: <u>R</u> A D O <u>N</u>

1. __ P R O __
2. __ N O W __
3. __ V A R __
4. __ X I S __
5. __ D I E __
6. __ H I P __
7. __ M U S __
8. __ I L K __
9. __ L O B __
10. __ W I S __
11. __ J U G __
12. __ W A S __
13. __ K I N __
14. __ U R N __
15. __ N A W __

16. __ I N S __
17. __ H E M __
18. __ L A X __
19. __ G I N __
20. __ C U T __
21. __ H O S E __
22. __ E A S T __
23. __ A C R O S S __
24. __ H E S T __
25. __ L I M A __
26. __ A T T I C __
27. __ D U C A T __
28. __ L E A R __
29. __ I N D I E S __
30. __ R A N K __

Split Ends Plus I

In this variation of Split Ends, add one letter to the beginning and one letter to the end of these words to make another ordinary word. You *may* use an "S" in the beginning or the end, provided that the "S" does not make the word plural.

Example: S C U L L E R Y

1. __ H I E S __
2. __ K I D D O __
3. __ E X P O __
4. __ O G L E S __
5. __ C R A W __
6. __ T A L K I E __
7. __ L O B B E R __
8. __ R A L E S __
9. __ C R E W __
10. __ T I N G L E S __
11. __ C R I B __
12. __ C A M P __
13. __ P A R E S __
14. __ M A R T __
15. __ E X I N E S __

16. __ H E A T __
17. __ H I V E __
18. __ T A R D O __
19. __ A U N T I E __
20. __ H A R P __
21. __ T H Y __
22. __ A F A R __
23. __ L A Y __
24. __ N I P __
25. __ A L I E N __
26. __ C U M M I N __
27. __ L A M I N G __
28. __ C O W __
29. __ H E C K L E S __
30. __ C H I N E S __

Expansion Joint

Keeping the letter sequence given, insert one letter in each word below to change it into another word. You may not add the letter to the beginning or to the end of the word.

Example: chorine, chlorine

1. BODIES
2. IMPERIL
3. ROUND
4. FALSE
5. MOODY
6. GENTLE
7. CORNEAL
8. MONEYED
9. HABITAT
10. HIDEOUS
11. IMPUDENT
12. BESIDE
13. PAYDAY
14. CURIOS
15. BELTED

16. MOUSE
17. TURKEY
18. EXCEPT
19. GOAD
20. MORALITY
21. BLUSTER
22. COSHED
23. WATERED
24. EXPIATION
25. DEPRECATE
26. CONTINENT
27. NUTRIENT
28. INSOLENT
29. ANTIRUST
30. FRESHEN

Whodunit

Become a word sleuth. Take one set of letters from the first column (A–Q) and add it to the beginning of a word in the second column (1–17) to form a new word.

Example: S T I N + G R A Y = Stingray

A. B A R S	1. __ A R T Y
B. B O R O	2. __ B L U E
C. C A R A	3. __ D I C E
D. C R O S	4. __ I L L Y
E. E A R P	5. __ L U G S
F. G H E T	6. __ O U R S
G. H A R B	7. __ O O Z E
H. J A U N	8. __ R A I D
I. M A H A	9. __ R A J A
J. N O N P	10. __ S W A Y
K. P R I N	11. __ T O E D
L. S C H M	12. __ T O O L
M. S H R E	13. __ T O U T
N. T R U E	14. __ U G H S
O. U N A F	15. __ U N I T
P. W E E V	16. __ V A N S
Q. W H O D	17. __ W I S H

Whodunit II

Become a word sleuth. Take one set of letters from the first column (A–Q) and add it to the beginning of a word in the second column (1–17) to form a new word.

Example: S T I N + G R A Y = Stingray

A. A L P H	1. __ A B E T
B. A N T I	2. __ B A N G
C. B L A S	3. __ C A P E
D. D O O R	4. __ C E E S
E. E P I S	5. __ E R G S
F. F I A N	6. __ E W E R
G. I C E B	7. __ F O R E
H. I N H U	8. __ J A M B
I. L O C K	9. __ J A W S
J. P A S T	10. __ M A L E
K. P I N A	11. __ M A N E
L. Q U A G	12. __ M I R E
M. R E V I	13. __ O D E S
N. S C R U	14. __ R A M I
O. S E A S	15. __ T E A R
P. W H E A	16. __ T I N Y
Q. W H I Z	17. __ T O F F

Whodunit III

Become a word sleuth. Take one set of letters from the first column (A–Q) and add it to the beginning of a word in the second (1–17) column to form a new word.

Example: S T I N + G R A Y = Stingray

A. B E N E	1. __ A I R Y
B. C R O S	2. __ A B Y E
C. D O M I	3. __ B I K E
D. F L Y S	4. __ B O N D
E. M I N I	5. __ C A R T
F. N O N D	6. __ F I S T
G. N O S E	7. __ F I T S
H. P A C I	8. __ G A Y S
I. P E I G	9. __ H A W K
J. P U S H	10. __ L A C S
K. R O C K	11. __ N O E S
L. S A N D	12. __ N O I R
M. S H E L	13. __ P E C K
N. T H E O	14. __ R E M S
O. T O M A	15. __ S C U T
P. T R U S	16. __ T E E D
Q. V A G A	17. __ W I C H

Whodunit IV

Become a word sleuth. Take one set of letters from the first column (A–Q) and add it to the beginning of a word in the second column (1–17) to form a new word.

Example: S T I N + G R A Y = Stingray

A.	A R M C	1.	__ A Z O N
B.	D I S O	2.	__ B A I T
C.	E M B L	3.	__ B E Y S
D.	E N S C	4.	__ D O F F
E.	J A I L	5.	__ E R N E
F.	M O N O	6.	__ G A Z E
G.	O U T B	7.	__ H A I R
H.	P L A S	8.	__ H I R E
I.	R E A T	9.	__ H O P S
J.	S A L I	10.	__ L A Z E
K.	S A P P	11.	__ N I T S
L.	S A U T	12.	__ O N C E
M.	S T A N	13.	__ P I A N
N.	S T A R	14.	__ P O L Y
O.	S U B U	15.	__ T A C H
P.	T E A S	16.	__ T I C S
Q.	T H E S	17.	__ V A R Y

Whodunit V

Become a word sleuth. Take one set of letters from the first column (A–Q) and add it to the beginning of a word in the second column (1–17) to form a new word.

Example: S T I N + G R A Y = Stingray

A. ALBA		1. __ AIDS
B. ASTE		2. __ AIRS
C. BARM		3. __ BIER
D. CHAP		4. __ BUTS
E. COCH		5. __ COMA
F. COUS		6. __ CORE
G. DRUG		7. __ DUAL
H. FLAB		8. __ DITS
I. FROS		9. __ GIST
J. GLAU		10. __ HERO
K. HALI		11. __ INLY
L. LOVE		12. __ KEYS
M. PLAU		13. __ LAIN
N. RANC		14. __ LILY
O. RESI		15. __ MORE
P. SYCA		16. __ RISK
Q. WHIS		17. __ TEDS

Expand each four- or five-letter word below by adding all the given letters to the front and back to form another word. The original word must remain unchanged within the newly formed word.

Example: T H E N + A C I T U = a u T H E N t i c
           M I T T + C E E M O = c o m M I T T e e

1. P O L E + A N N O = _____

2. D O M E + E O R T = _____

3. R O S E + E E K N = _____

4. A C H E + B L O R = _____

5. H A N G + A H I S = _____

6. K N O T + A B E N = _____

7. R I N G + E E M U = _____

8. R A F F + G I I T = _____

9. P A R T + A D E H I = _____

10. I N S E T + A I O P T = _____

11. T I N E + A I R R Y = _____

12. T E R M + A D I M N S = _____

13. T E N + I L S U = _____

14. S I L O + E N P = _____

15. R I O T + A C I P T = _____

eYESight II

Expand each four- or five-letter word by adding all the given letters to the front and back to form another word. The original word must remain unchanged within the newly formed word.

Example: F E T E + A A C I R = c a F E T E r i a
R A T E + G S T Y = s t R A T E g y

1. M I E N + I O P T = _____

2. R E I N + E H O T = _____

3. R O S E + C E P T U = _____

4. B R A N + E E M M = _____

5. H A N G + A C E L R = _____

6. P A G A N + A D O P R = _____

7. L O V E + A C E F L R = _____

8. T I L E + O S T T = _____

9. Q U I T + M O O S = _____

10. F O R T + C E M O R = _____

11. R O M P + I M P T U = _____

12. T E R M + A A F H T = _____

13. T I C + C I I M R S = _____

14. S P A R + A A G S U = _____

15. C O H O + A C I L L = _____

eYESight III

Expand each four- or five-letter word by adding all the given letters to the front and back to form another word. The original word must remain unchanged within the newly formed word.

Example: R E A D + I L L M T = t R E A D m i l l
          M I N I + C E E R S = r e M I N I s c e

1. C H I N + E I S S T = _____

2. C H E S T + A O R R = _____

3. H A L E + A D M R S = _____

4. S E N T + D E R Y Y = _____

5. P A S T + A I N O T = _____

6. L I O N + H I L M T = _____

7. R A P E + A P S T = _____

8. L O C K + A B D E = _____

9. H A R M + A C P Y = _____

10. H A I R + A C M N = _____

11. C R I B + A E S S = _____

12. L A T E + A P U = _____

13. T H Y + A E M S T = _____

14. R O W + B E I N S = _____

15. U S E + B H O O Y = _____

eYESight IV

Expand each three- or four-letter word below by adding all the given letters to the front and back to form another word. The original word must remain unchanged within the newly formed word.

Example: R E A D + O O R T = t o R E A D o r
           L E S T + A C E I L = c e L E S T i a l

1. N O W + I S S U T = _____

2. C A R + A I M N O = _____

3. A R M + A C E K R = _____

4. O W N + A B D E T = _____

5. R U D E + I M N P T = _____

6. T H I N + I K M S = _____

7. P O T + E I M N S = _____

8. N U T + E I M S T = _____

9. F I G + G H N T U = _____

10. P O L O + G O T Y = _____

11. N I N E + I S S T = _____

12. H E R + E O P R S U = _____

13. L I E N + C E E L T = _____

14. B L E W + A A E R T = _____

15. S T A B + E L N U = _____

Expert eYESight
Only for those with extremely keen vision!

Expand each word below by adding all the given letters to the front and back to form another word. The original word must remain unchanged within the newly formed word.

Example:
 M E M O + A C E M O R T = c o m MEMO r a t e
 A-L I S T + C I I R T U = r i t u ALIST i c

1. S C O N C E + I I M N O P T = _____

2. T I C + A E I L P P R = _____

3. U N D E R + A C H L P T = _____

4. T I M E + C E E N R T = _____

5. A N T I + C E E L R V = _____

6. S E W + E F H I O U = _____

7. D E N S + A C E N O T = _____

8. H Y D R A + A B C E O R T = _____

9. B A R D + B E I M O R = _____

10. P O S T + A E H O P R = _____

11. L I F E + A E O P R R T = _____

12. THEMATIC + AAIMN = _____

• Puns & Anagrams •

Joyce Shtick—Hospital

Hidden within each sentence below is a word or phrase relating to a hospital. Cryptic crossword puzzle fans may already be familiar with the types of word play used—anagrams, homophones, puns, and hidden words. To get you started, the first answer is *ambulance*, an anagram of the words *male Cuban*. The number of letters for the answer is in parentheses.

1. The confused patient transported in the emergency vehicle is a male Cuban. (9)

2. I see you are getting very special care in the hospital. (3)

3. Sir, grey is the color of the standard operating gown. (7)

4. Well, I want something un-grey, especially when I'm on that stretcher. (6)

5. The doctor-in-training will see each of you in turn. (6)

6. A "D," miss? I only give service in the entering area a "D" rating. (9)

7. Ray's room is right after section W. (4) (4)

8. May I rent this crib until I can buy one? (9)

9. Gene, mercy! Call the nurse immediately! (9)

10. I can sue, R.N.; so, you'd better have proper coverage. (9)

Joyce Shtick—Paris

Hidden within each sentence below is a word or phrase relating to Paris. Cryptic crossword puzzle fans may already be familiar with the types of word play used—anagrams, homophones, puns, and hidden words. To get you started, the first answer is *Seine*, a homophone of *sane*. The number of letters for the answer is in parentheses.

1. It is not sane, I hear, cruising in a *bateau-mouche!* (5)

2. When walking down this boulevard, try the cheesy samples some of the cafés offer. (6) (7)

3. Travel royally, the layout is worth the small amount of confusion. (4)

4. The velour drapes were not suited to the art display. (3) (6)

5. If you have time for it, leisure strolls through the gardens are romantic. (9)

6. Having time trouble? It can be the quickest route! (5)

7. The stained-glass windows are not red. A meander down the aisle will reveal glorious colors. (5) (4)

8. So, animal lover, smile! (4) (4)

9. At noon, leap on the tour bus and learn about this great Frenchman. (8)

10. When the trip is over, sail less, enjoy fabulous sights. (10)

11. The tour guide's name was, strangely, Quartarius. (5) (7)

Joyce Shtick—High School

Hidden within each sentence below is a word relating to a high school. Cryptic crossword puzzle fans may already be familiar with the types of word play used—anagrams, homophones, puns, and hidden words. To get you started, the first answer is *computer*, sit*com put Er*ica. The number of letters for the answer is in parentheses.

1. In acting class, a sitcom put Erica at the keyboard. (8)

2. Two bewildered Maxes took the biology finals. (5)

3. Jim thinks one must be athletic to be a well-rounded student. (3)

4. Subtract the "D" and that confounded subject is gradable. (7)

5. She confusedly trimmed her nails before taking the typing test. (7)

6. Arthur would rather use a brush than a ballpoint. (3)

7. Shakespeare did well in this and mistakenly thought he should hang out his shingle. (7)

8. A knowledge of wingspan is helpful when studying physics in Madrid. (7)

9. Unclear sign on blackboard: "SNs teaming to do the task." (10)

10. Likely to catch a cheater! (7)

11. "C" in your name? Register in row three if this is your last year. (6)

12. Sachem is trying to learn the periodic table. (9)

Joyce Shtick—Visiting the Zoo

Hidden within each sentence below is a word relating to zoo inhabitants. Cryptic crossword puzzle fans may already be familiar with the types of word play used—anagrams, homophones, puns, and hidden words. The number of letters for the answer is in parentheses.

1. Did you see the baby bird trapped in the towel? (5)

2. I don't think a raptor describes that kind of bird. (6)

3. A very agile muralist must have painted the arboreal mammal on the ceiling of the main entry hall. (5)

4. Did your aunt elope and take that African trip? (8)

5. Does Veronica R. want to meet me by the meat eater? (9)

6. Is that bird's plumage really flaming orange? (8)

7. Why is Kay sneaking up on that viper? (9)

8. Has Pa ten of those feathers from the game bird? (8)

9. The wading bird's foreleg retains that color of feathers into adulthood. (5)

10. That mammal complains loudly if put in a bare cage. (4)

11. This reptile is a real maniac! (6)

12. That animal eats too slowly when given the rootiest plants. (8)

13. Before strolling to the other habitat, let's see the deer. (6)

Joyce Shtick—Joy of Foods

Hidden within each sentence below is a word relating to foods or food preparation. Cryptic crossword puzzle fans may already be familiar with the types of word play used— anagrams, homophones, puns, and hidden words. The number of letters for the answer is in parentheses.

1. Didn't Rose marry the herb gardener? (8)

2. This crustacean treat will bolster your spirits. (7)

3. There wasn't a soul in the seafood restaurant. (4)

4. Ha! Novices eat their pizza plain. They're wrong! (9)

5. You must stay in the room to stir and thicken the sauce. (7)

6. Don't have the crab alone; serve it with another shell-fish. (7)

7. Don't order your sandwich from that deli; it does deliver worst! (10)

8. Following this diet regimen, you must avoid certain lemon pies. (8)

9. Pairs of these with cottage cheese are good low-calorie lunches. (5)

10. Take Mary's word, fish *is* brain food. (9)

11. A bear hug! Mr. Tangled gave me one at the barbecue. (9)

12. We can catch up on news while eating our fries. (7)

13. Even though the vegetables are assembled with art, I choke on large pieces of this one. (9)

Joyce Shtick—A Day at the Office

Hidden within each sentence below is a word relating to a day at work in an office. Cryptic crossword puzzle fans may already be familiar with the types of word play used— anagrams, homophones, puns, and hidden words. The number of letters for the answer is in parentheses.

1. Did Pat mention P. Jenkins was interviewing her at 4 P.M.? (11)

2. Is that the right coiffe for a white-collar job? (11)

3. If they were organized, the crystal factory wouldn't be so messy. Stemware here, there, and everywhere! (6)

4. It's a cinch; add 50 and you'll do this to the deal! (6)

5. She predates the use of Lotus 123 at this office! (11)

6. To be practical, end around the last day of each month. (8)

7. They're like the gestapo, watching every stamp I use! (7)

8. Without a fax machine, are you keeping your board of directors informed? (8)

9. The typewriter works well except for the "S," which sticks when you turn it on. (6)

10. She counted 1,000 pieces of paper as evidence for that case. (8)

11. That's right! Some authors do this better than others! (5)

Word Doodles & Alphacryptics

About Word Doodles

These visual puns use symbols, placement, size, shape, and style to convey various words or concepts. They can represent phrases, sayings, titles, names, places, and so forth. Here are some examples.

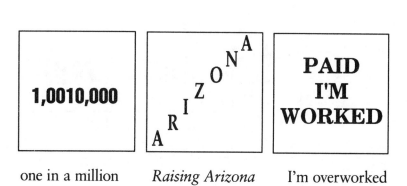

one in a million Raising Arizona I'm overworked
and underpaid.

Cooking Class

Decipher these word doodles which represent kitchen and menu items. *Bon appétit!*

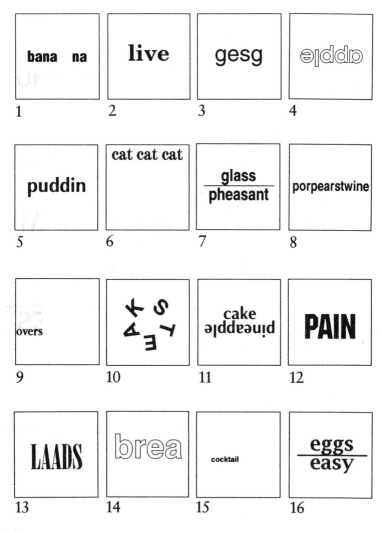

bana na	**live**	gesg	ǝlddɐ
1	2	3	4

cat cat cat		glass / pheasant	
puddin			porpearstwine
5	6	7	8

overs		cake / ǝlddɐǝuᴉd	**PAIN**
9	10	11	12

LAADS	brea	cocktail	eggs / easy
13	14	15	16

Songs & Musical Compositions

Decipher these word doodles which represent the names of well-known songs and musical compositions.

1. STAND ME

2. MY WINGS / WIND

3. SYMPHO

4. noel noel noel noel noel noel noel (repeated)

5. TU/LOI⌁PS

6. THEUBORNSA

7. MOON SONATA

8. GOLDEN GATE / TWSERA

9. HOPES

Decipher these word doodles which represent popular television shows. Most are American shows.

1. HOUSE / PRAIRIE

2. RAH! OLÉ! BRAVO!

3. (circle) SUCCESSWEALTHLOVEGOODLUCKHAPPINESSHEALTH

4. oursoursoursoursours (repeated)

5. STAIRS (arranged in arch shape)

6. POTATO CHOCOLATE WOOD

7. NIGHTNIGHTNIGHT (vertical)

8. Murder

9. PRICE (vertical)

People

Decipher these word doodles which represent the names of famous people.

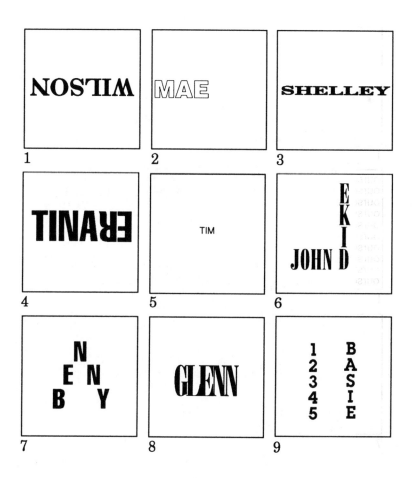

1

2

3

4

5

6

7

8

9

Decipher these word doodles which represent famous American movies.

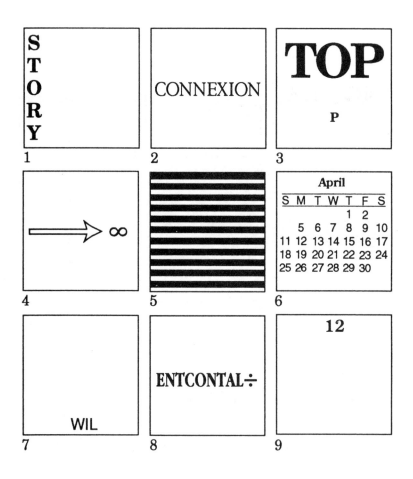

Matinee II

Decipher these word doodles which represent famous American movies.

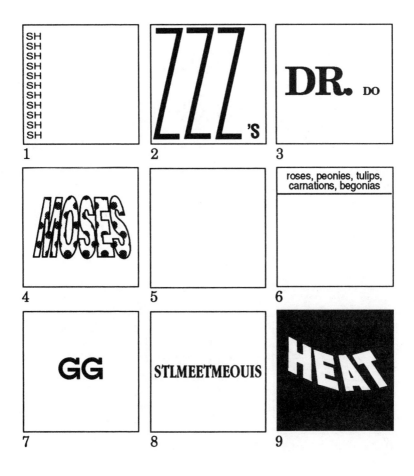

1.
```
SH
SH
SH
SH
SH
SH
SH
SH
SH
SH
SH
```

2.
ZZZ's

3.
DR. DO

4.
MOSES

5.

6.
roses, peonies, tulips, carnations, begonias

7.
GG

8.
STLMEETMEOUIS

9.
HEAT

Matinee III

Decipher these word doodles which represent famous American movies.

JOHN WAYNE JIMMY CARTER KEVIN COSTNER and MAGGIE SIMPSON 1	**DEATH & TAXES** 2	3:14 PM, 4:21 PM 3
CIRCUI 4	TA BLES 5	PAGANINI ROOF 6
ON OR ABOUT JUNE 22 7	ALL ALLALLALL ALLALLEVEALLALL ALLALLALL ALL 8	9

Book Club

Decipher these word doodles which represent titles of famous works. We've given you the authors' names to help you; match the rebus with the author and title.

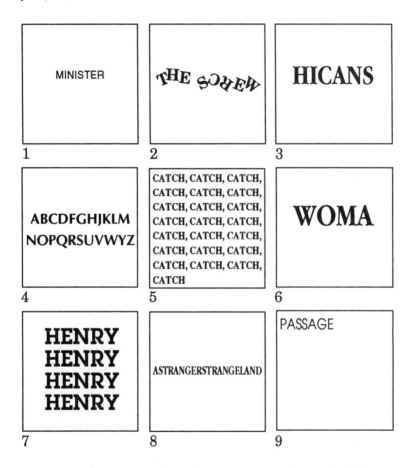

Joseph Heller, Kenneth Roberts, James M. Barrie, Henry James, Jean-Paul Sartre, William Shakespeare, Lillian Hellman, Robert Heinlein, James Fenimore Cooper

Book Club II

Decipher these word doodles which represent titles of famous works. We've given you the authors' names to help you; match the rebus with the author and title.

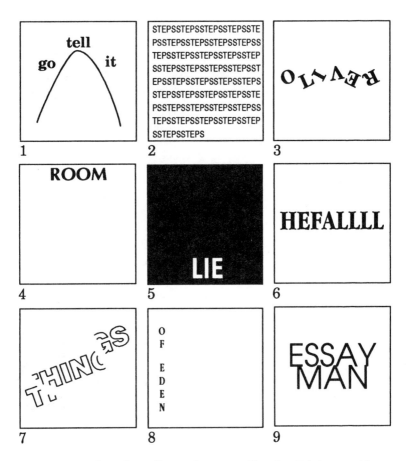

Arthur Rimbaud, William Styron, Charles Dickens, Alexander Pope, John Braine, Chinua Achebe, John Steinbeck, James Baldwin, John Buchan

Book Club III

Decipher these word doodles which represent titles of famous works. We've given you the authors' names to help you; match the rebus with the author and title.

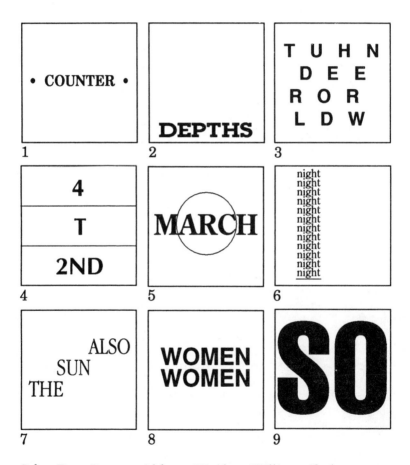

John Dos Passos, Aldous Huxley, William Shakespeare, Alberto Moravia, Ernest Hemingway, Edna Ferber, Maxim Gorky, Fyodor Dostoevski, George Eliot

Book Club IV

Decipher these word doodles which represent titles of famous works. We've given you the authors' names to help you; match the rebus with the author and title.

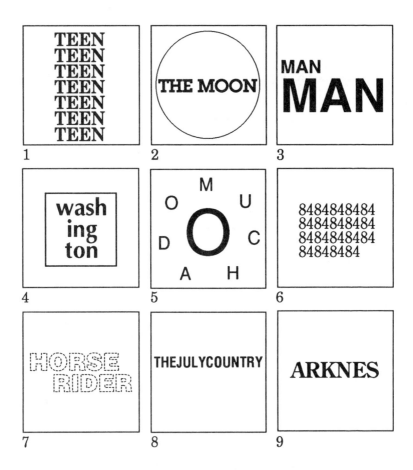

Ivan Turgenev, Booth Tarkington, George Orwell, George Bernard Shaw, Katherine Anne Porter, Joseph Conrad, Henry James, William Shakespeare, Jean Anouilh

Alphacryptics

Look carefully to see if you can determine the word or phrase suggested by the alphabet strings below. Confused? The first answer is *nohow* (no H, O, or W); #2 is *fatback* or *finback* (F at back). You're on your own!

1. A B C D E F G I J K L M N P Q R S T U V X Y Z

2. A B C D E G H I J K L M N O P Q R S T U V W X Y Z F

3. A B C D F G H I J K L M N Q S T U V W X Y Z

4. A B C D E F G H I K L M N P Q R S T U V W X Z

5. A B C D **E** F G H **I** J K **L** M N O P Q R S T U V W X Y Z

6. Ⓐ Ⓐ B Ⓒ D Ⓔ F G H I J K L Ⓜ N O P Q Ⓡ S T U V W X Y Z

7. A B C D E F G H I √ J K L M N √ O √ P √ Q R S T √ U V W X Y Z

8. A B C D E F H J L P Q R T U V W X Y Z

9. A Ⓑ C D E F G H Ⓘ J K L M Ⓝ Ⓞ P Q Ⓡ S T U V W X Y Z

10. A B C D E F G H I J K L M N o p Q R S T U V W x Y Z

Alphacryptics II

Look carefully to see if you can determine the word or phrase suggested by these alphabet strings.

1. E E O R S T

2. A B C D E F G H I J K L M N O P Q R S T U V W X
   Y Z   A D Y

3. A B C D F G H J K L N O P Q R U V W X Y Z E I
   M S T ←

4. a B C D E F G H I J K L m n o P Q R S T U V w X Y
   Z

5. B A C D F E S H L J N K G M O P Q R T U V I S W
   X Y Z

6. A B B C D E F G H I J K L M N O P Q R S T U V W
   X Y Z

7. Ⓐ B Ⓒ Ⓓ Ⓔ F G H I J K L M Ⓝ O P Q R S T U V W
   X Y Z

8. C H O P R A B D E F G I J K L M N Q S T U V W X
   Y Z

9. A B C D D E F G H I J K L M N O P Q R S T T U U
   V W X Y Z

10. E O R V A B C D F G H I J K L M N P Q S T U W X
    Y Z

40

• Word Meaning •

Double Identities

Many people's names are also acceptable ordinary words or terms. Below are the definitions of the first and last names of famous people. Test your vocabulary and discover who they are.

Example: irregular plural of term describing dark, flat areas of moon; lilies described breathlessly by Hepburn   <u>Maria</u> <u>Callas</u>

1. policeman's club; fine glassware

   _____   _____

2. pungent root often used as a spice; plural of radio term indicating message received

   _____   _____

3. hereditary unit; more primitive or unrestrained

   _____   _____

4. long, thick nail often used on railroads; shelter from the wind _____   _____

5. male cat; skeins of yarn _____   _____

6. mollusk-made gem; male deer

   _____   _____

7. honey; babbling streams _____   _____

8. a drugged drink; shelf above fireplace

   _____   _____

Double Identities II

Many people's names are also acceptable ordinary words or terms. Below are the definitions of the first and last names of famous people. Test your vocabulary and discover who they are.

Example: to hunt or chase; to pursue in order to capture or overtake   <u>Chevy</u> <u>Chase</u>

1. a sleeveless hospital gown; ready money in currency or coin _____ _____

2. holiday evergreen with red berries; one who pursues game for food or sport _____ _____

3. college official responsible for enforcing rules; bird, usually preceded by *purple* or *house*

   _____ _____

4. baby kangaroo; chesspiece which moves diagonally

   _____ _____

5. aesthetically meaningful rearrangement of materials; one who works in a carnival

   _____ _____

6. to droop or become limp; official who manages a nobleman's household _____ _____

7. informal name for a cat; bright green color

   _____ _____

8. seemingly effortless charm; smooth or slippery, often said of ice _____ _____

9. solidified animal or vegetable oils; a black-and-white-spotted game piece _____ _____

Double Identities III

Many people's names are also acceptable ordinary words or terms. Below are the definitions of the first and last names of famous people. Test your vocabulary and discover who they are.

Example: to raise with a lever, often a car; a champion (British dialect) <u>Jack</u> <u>Kemp</u>

1. deep red precious stone; the letter "D"
   _____ _____

2. to issue forth from a defensive position; a cultivated expanse of land _____ _____

3. to slowly come to an end, dwindle; wolf-like North American carnivorous mammal
   _____ _____

4. a type of blackbird; worn and exhausted appearance, gaunt _____ _____

5. one who wins the spoils; having reached full growth or development _____ _____

6. one who leaves a gratuity for a waiter; to pierce with a horn _____ _____

7. Scotch for *soul* or *mettle*; a bull's very loud cry
   _____ _____

8. slang for amphetamine tablet; archaic for master of the household (used in Salem)
   _____ _____

9. from French, a male sweetheart; structures erected over waterways _____ _____

Equivokes

Determine the proper definition for these words.

1. NIGHTJAR
   a. a type of chamber pot
   b. any of a genus of bird related to the whippoorwill
   c. a container for cleansing cream

2. SKYHOOK
   a. a hook conceived as being suspended from the sky
   b. a showy flying maneuver
   c. an astronomical configuration

3. LONGHEAD
   a. a highbrow
   b. a long-skulled person
   c. an avid fan of classical music

4. HELLBOX
   a. a derisive name for television used by theatre owners
   b. a backstage waiting area for performers
   c. a printer's receptacle for discarded type

5. DUTCHMAN
   a. something used to hide structural defects
   b. a type of door
   c. a nautical term for a missing ship

6. EARLOCK
   a. a sailor's knot resembling an ear
   b. a curl of hair by the ear
   c. a regional variation of the word *oarlock*

7. SUPERSEX
   a. a sterile organism having both male and female characteristics

b. feminist coining for the female sex
c. of a sexually satisfying nature

8. SMEARCASE
   a. mechanic's case for storing oily tools before cleaning
   b. a type of cottage cheese
   c. a container for theatrical makeup

9. DAYMARE
   a. horse used as a pacer for morning workouts at race tracks
   b. a nightmarish fantasy experienced while awake
   c. a type of weather characteristic of the horse latitudes

10. DRAGÉE
    a. a member of the Indian elite classes
    b. a sugar-coated nut
    c. something which is transported by dragging

11. TAPSTER
    a. a tap dancer
    b. a tavern keeper or bartender
    c. one engaged in illegal phone surveillance

12. CATCHFLY
    a. an insect-trapping plant
    b. a net behind home plate in baseball stadiums
    c. a bowl of sugared water used in colonial kitchens to trap flies

13. WARMOUTH
    a. an aggressive person
    b. a hawkish or right-wing newspaper
    c. a freshwater fish

Equivokes II

Determine the proper definition for these words.

1. FILMSET
   a. related to photocomposition
   b. members of the motion picture industry
   c. diaphanous scrim used by photographers

2. TOPCROSS
   a. a cross mounted on a steeple
   b. a skiing maneuver
   c. a cross between a purebred male and inferior female stock

3. RIPRAP
   a. to strengthen with a foundation of broken stones
   b. a type of saw
   c. a particularly strong riptide feared by surfers

4. CANFIELD
   a. a garbage dump
   b. a metallic coated arena used by skateboarders
   c. a type of card game

5. PEDIPALP
   a. an orthopedic device
   b. sensory appendage of an arachnid
   c. a type of foot-powered vehicle

6. COYDOG
   a. a hybrid between a coyote and a wild dog
   b. a dog trained to be used in undercover police work, particularly narcotics investigations
   c. a sly person

7. FOOTLER
    a. an inexperienced male servant
    b. one who wastes time
    c. a measuring device used in shoe manufacturing

8. PALETOT
    a. a loose overcoat
    b. an anemic child
    c. a poor financial showing

9. CHAINMAN
    a. a convict
    b. a surveyor's assistant
    c. a specialty trade in jewelry making

10. FLOPOVER
    a. a defect in television reception
    b. a type of omelet
    c. a fast profit made on a commodity exchange by buying and selling almost simultaneously

11. GAPOSIS
    a. coined by *Time* magazine, an information gap
    b. a dental problem characterized by a gap between front incisors
    c. a gap in a row of buttons or snaps

12. BEESWING
    a. a crust on the surface of some old wines
    b. a two-seater swing shaped like the letter "B"
    c. a lightweight wing used on small aircraft

13. QUEENSIDE
    a. the seat placed to the right of a dignitary at formal gatherings, indicating a place of honor
    b. the side of the chessboard containing the file on which the queen sits at the start of a chess game
    c. the port side of a ship, from British naval tradition

• Trivia Word Search •

Ziggurat

Find the name, phrase, or word beginning with the letter "Z" which fits the definitions below. The answers are also hidden in the maze which follows, *except all the Z's have been removed*. The words can be traced, using any adjacent letters, whether above, below, beside, or diagonal to. *No letter can be used more than once*, and there are no extra letters. Your answer may zigzag through the maze. Obviously, you can also use the maze to find answers you may be uncertain about.

1. From German, meaning the spirit of the time

2. Strangely spelled teething rusk

3. Character in many horror movies

4. Nothing, zero

5. Drought-resistant grass

6. Led ———————, "Stairway to Heaven"

7. Swiss city

8. His follies made him famous. (last name)

9. Spaceman's weightlessness

10. *Viva* this Mexican revolutionary!

11. "Top of the line" American appliance?

12. A photographer would probably have this.

13. A gentle breeze
14. Prolific garden vegetable
15. Originally Zone Improvement Plan
16. Describing an abundantly endowed female
17. Dry red table wine
18. Retro (1940s) men's wear
19. "Religion" of the Beat Generation
20. Movement which led to establishment of Israel

E	R	R	I	N	E	L	T	M	S
O	G	A	V	F	D	I	O	N	I
A	Y	T	I	A	N	U	I	M	S
P	A	T	A	E	O	S	D	H	I
E	N	S	O	D	O	T	D	U	B
T	I	N	C	F	T	I	G	E	N
H	E	I	P	A	H	I	I	L	D
O	L	U	C	C	R	N	I	E	H
O	M	E	P	H	Y	F	N	I	C
E	I	B	M	I	E	G	I	U	R
G	E	I	O	I	L	C	L	E	P
I	T	S	B	A	K	H	S	I	P
E	T	W	I	E	C	O	Y	A	E

"Y" Knot

The answers to these trivia questions all begin with the letter "Y." When you've figured out the answers, look for them in the maze below. *All the Y's have been removed from the words.* The words in the maze can be traced, using any adjacent letters, whether above, below, beside, or diagonal. *No letter can be used more than once,* and there are no extra letters. Your answer may zigzag through the maze. Obviously, you can also use the maze to find answers you may be uncertain about.

1. Home of Old Faithful

2. Great dance song by The Village People

3. Disease which hindered building the Panama Canal

4. Flowering plant whose dried stalks are sometimes used to cast the *I Ching*

5. Scene of historical conference in February 1945, attended by Stalin, Churchill, and Roosevelt

6. Irish poet, playwright, winner of Nobel Prize, 1923 (full name)

7. Classic English accompaniment to roast beef

8. Day of atonement

9. Song popular during the American Revolution

10. Passive female principle and active masculine principle in Chinese philosophy

11. A Hindu discipline which involves a stylized system of exercise to promote control of mind and body

12. Cultured milk product

13. A Japanese dish consisting of skewered and grilled pieces of chicken

14. Country at the southwestern tip of the Arabian peninsula

15. Neil Simon play, *Lost in* _____

16. A one-year-old thoroughbred race horse

17. Christmas time

E	S	E	E	L	D	E	E	P	I
M	R	U	K	D	O	K	U	P	K
E	L	G	N	O	I	N	R	M	O
N	E	N	O	G	N	A	A	I	L
E	T	I	A	O	A	B	M	I	L
D	I	L	N	A	N	U	W	O	W
E	A	R	G	D	L	T	A	R	R
R	I	T	O	G	E	T	A	W	A
O	T	R	G	N	R	L	F	O	L
I	K	U	I	A	E	E	E	E	L
A	U	D	D	T	R	V	E	S	W
P	R	S	K	S	A	N	T	L	O
E	I	H	R	O	C	M	O	L	E

OD'd on "O"

The answers to these trivia questions are words or phrases which all begin with the letter "O." When you've determined the answers, you can look for them in the letter maze which follows. *All the initial O's have been removed from the words in the maze.* The words in the maze can be traced, using any adjacent letters, whether above, below, beside, or diagonal to. *No letter can be used more than once*, and there are no extra letters. Your answer may zigzag through the maze. Obviously, you can also use the maze to help you find answers you may be uncertain about.

1. Historic overland route to the West, beginning at the Missouri River

2. Beloved of Eurydice

3. Filmdom's top award

4. Titania's husband (*Midsummer Night's Dream*)

5. Remote Australian countryside

6. Exotic flower

7. Athletic happening in 1996, 2000, 2004

8. Pertaining to the sense of smell

9. Unfortunately related to Jocasta

10. Venerable English university

11. Planned _____, outmoded on purpose

12. Roman poet, author of *Ars Amatoria*

13. Did he act alone on November 22, 1963? (full name)

14. Was Dogpatch located in these hilly uplands of Missouri?

15. To kiss

16. Collectively, islands of Central and South Pacific

17. The Sooner state

18. In Egyptian mythology, god of the underworld, husband-brother of Isis

Y	S	W	S	U	L	A	S	R	S
E	V	A	C	L	K	H	I	I	A
L	R	L	D	A	A	I	O	M	D
E	A	A	R	T	E	N	A	R	O
E	H	Z	K	S	C	E	S	X	F
C	E	N	V	I	Y	P	U	S	I
S	E	C	E	D	R	I	D	C	P
L	O	S	B	T	O	E	L	Y	M
L	F	A	C	B	E	N	H	P	R
D	I	A	B	R	O	E	R	T	O
H	C	C	T	A	S	U	A	N	G
R	K	U	R	C	S	L	I	R	E

Valedictorian

The answers to these trivia questions all begin with the letter "V." When you've figured out the answers, look for them again in the letter maze which follows. *All the initial V's have been removed from the words in the maze.* The words can be traced, using any adjacent letters, whether above, below, beside, or diagonal. *No letter can be used more than once*, and there are no extra letters. Your answer may zigzag through the maze. You can also use the maze to find answers you may be uncertain about.

1. Profession of James Herriot
2. Animal having a backbone
3. Mistress of Merlin (the Lady of the Lake)
4. Composer of *The Four Seasons*
5. Anne Rice antihero
6. Nature abhors this
7. Subject of many Chevy Chase movies
8. Satirical Thackeray novel
9. Setting of *Romeo and Juliet*
10. May 8th, 1945
11. International United States government radio
12. A master of technique in the arts
13. Police division charged with combatting prostitution, gambling
14. Another name for a snake

15. A tramp

16. Papal seat in Rome

17. "Dizzy" Hitchcock film

18. Late-afternoon or evening prayers

19. Enjoyed as a result of imaginary participation

20. Eating predilection of G. B. Shaw

V	I	F	A	M	I	V	A	L	I
I	N	O	E	R	I	R	T	D	I
A	I	E	C	I	S	O	U	E	P
O	C	A	E	R	O	E	R	R	I
E	R	T	E	T	E	T	I	R	A
O	G	I	S	P	B	E	N	A	N
A	F	Y	O	E	R	A	T	E	E
I	Y	T	N	I	R	S	N	O	R
R	A	I	A	T	M	U	A	E	G
E	D	N	A	C	A	U	A	T	E
C	A	R	I	A	C	E	R	I	A
I	Q	U	O	N	T	R	N	A	N
S	E	A	U	A	R	I	M	C	T
I	C	D	S	A	G	P	A	I	A

T Square

The answers to the following trivia questions all begin with the letter "T." When you've found the answers, find them again in the letter maze which follows. *All the initial T's have been removed from the words in the maze.* The words can be traced, using adjoining letters whether above, below, beside or diagonal. *No letter can be used more than once,* and there are no extra letters. You can also use the maze to find answers you may be uncertain about.

1. Christian holiday celebrated on January 5th

2. An English square

3. It's a devil

4. Yolky painting medium

5. Shores in Marine Corps anthem

6. Transportation to a beheading

7. In a teapot?

8. John Gotti, the _____ Don

9. Toy named after a U.S. President

10. *Rex* of *Jurassic Park*

11. "She sells seashells" is one

12. Caused by the Helen-Paris fling

13. Thor Heyerdahl's Kon

14. Every three years

15. Male hormone

16. Provable proposition in math

17. Landed Dorothy in Oz

18. Archipelago at extreme tip of South America, "land of fire"

19. Opposed to Whig

20. Gulf, northwestern arm of the China Sea, pivotal in United States history

E	S	T	A	D	D	E	L	N	N
T	S	O	N	O	A	E	F	I	E
E	R	O	R	R	O	G	U	A	I
E	N	O	O	R	O	N	L	R	R
H	E	R	E	E	K	I	R	Y	A
R	A	W	M	I	N	O	I	B	E
J	A	N	E	T	I	K	Y	D	D
R	O	R	W	I	S	P	O	L	E
G	U	E	R	U	S	I	R	A	I
O	N	S	A	U	U	R	E	P	M
N	N	O	O	N	M	G	A	R	E
A	R	L	L	R	B	L	A	F	A
Y	E	F	E	A	M	G	H	T	R
S	E	P	N	N	S	I	T	F	L
T	E	M	A	I	A	N	H	W	E

• Relatively Speaking •

My Cousin Charley

My cousin Charley loves words and word play. Everything he does centers around words, word patterns, puns, and general tomfoolery having to do with dictionaries and word guides. Discover some of his quirks and unmask the word tricks in these sentences. In the first sentence, for example, the words *dialogue* and *euphoria* contain all the vowels—*a, e, i, o, u.*

1. He can dialogue with euphoria, but he cannot discourse with enthusiasm.

2. He named his cats Munster and Sternum, rejecting our suggestions of Monster and Stewbum.

3. He reads *Moby Dick* but not *Billy Budd.* He loves *Jane Eyre* but hates *Wuthering Heights.*

4. He will wear chinos but not khakis. He will listen to a cello but not to a bass viola. He will believe a ghost is in the house but definitely will not accept the thought of an apparition.

5. He loves the cancan but hates French dancing. He loves a good bonbon but hates candy.

6. He bids "adieu" but won't say "goodbye." He keeps his clothes in a bureau but won't use a dresser.

7. He will pout when he has the gout and complain when he has a pain, but he won't fuss over his health.

Charley's Cats

When my cousin Charley got his new cats, Munster and Sternum, he nearly drove us mad. For months he sprinkled his conversation with nine-letter words (for nine lives, get it?) containing the word *cat*. Of course, there were big gaps in his speech while he searched his encyclopedic vocabulary for the right word for each occasion. Try to extriCATe from the clues below the nine-letter words Charley used to give us all CATalepsy.

1. The only kind of church he would go into was a
   _____.

2. His sailboat was a specific kind, a _____.

3. He wouldn't drink rieslings, or any other wines but
   _____.

4. He did not utter an obscenity, but instead became obsessed with _____.

5. Quite the athlete, Charley participated in a
   _____.

6. He didn't chew his food, he would only _____ it.

7. When he needed new glasses, he told us he hoped he wasn't developing _____.

8. When he took his pills, Charley told us he was now properly _____.

9. Worried about a breathing problem the cats had, Charley told us that they would not _____.

10. He wouldn't oil his car, he would _____ it.

Charley's Aunts

My cousin Charley had a strange relationship with the rest of the family. To find out how you stood with him, you had to be great at anagrams. For years, he blithely called one of his mother's sisters *Aunt Eased* until she figured out Charley's nickname for her was an anagram for *nauseated*. Find the anagram of these aunts' names to discover the hidden quality, trait, or occupation which piqued Charley's interest.

1. AUNT HERHED worked for an employment agency.

2. AUNT GROAN had a very simian appearance.

3. AUNT CLORN never went out during the day.

4. AUNT PROMA worked for a major motion picture studio.

5. AUNT SERES loved fine wines.

6. AUNT CORER told a great story.

7. AUNT BLERT used to be a deejay.

8. AUNT FADIR once worked for Ralph Nader.

9. AUNT LEFTL was not a person you wanted to be in an enclosed space with.

10. AUNT ALTAR was hairy and scary.

11. AUNT DEBET once had a coming-out party.

12. AUNT BODIC was once kidnapped.

13. AUNT ASTOR was very spacey.

14. AUNT DENNS always wintered in Florida.

Charley's Uncles

Charley's uncles, like most of the aunts, never figured out what Charley thought about them. *Uncle Meow* never knew the letters in his nickname were an anagram for *unwelcome*. Here's your chance to uncover family secrets. Find the anagrams of the uncles' names to discover the quality, trait, or occupation which Charley hid.

1. UNCLE ICY used an unusual mode of transportation.

2. UNCLE AIRT chewed a lot of Tums.

3. UNCLE PORT could stand to lose a few pounds.

4. UNCLE BANDA couldn't walk a straight line, even when sober.

5. UNCLE KISS won the lottery.

6. UNCLE AMIS thought he was very manly.

7. UNCLE THIM loved to eat at noon.

8. UNCLE AMBA was very accident-prone.

9. UNCLE AITH, the lawyer, was something of a shyster.

10. UNCLE DORS was an unprincipled rascal.

11. UNCLE SCUT was "full of juice."

12. UNCLE RESS was downright mean.

13. UNCLE FAFE had more money than anyone else in the family.

14. UNCLE ORSO was always dispensing unwanted advice.

Cousinly

The cousins, of course, fit into Charley's anagram scheme. *Cousin DT*, an anagram for the word *discount*, liked to shop for bargains. See if you can determine why Charley gave the nicknames below to the rest of his large tribe of cousins. Figure out the anagrams of the cousins' names to make sense of Charley's cousin-naming game.

1. COUSIN SIP works as a detective.

2. COUSIN URI was always very uninterested.

3. COUSIN LES wants to be alone.

4. COUSIN RET comes from a long line of eccentrics who could use a little psychoanalysis.

5. COUSIN REX loves trips.

6. COUSIN TAD spends a lot of time with broomsticks.

7. COUSIN G. T. loves camporees.

8. COUSIN TED is quite the ladies' man.

9. COUSIN OLL likes to plot with other people in illegal schemes. He's been in jail.

10. COUSIN V. T. is an English nobleman.

11. COUSIN FON is really bewildering.

12. COUSIN TEA is very dogged.

13. COUSIN GAR loves to party.

14. COUSIN LIN is always saying, "Count me in!"

15. COUSIN TENTO loves to fight.

Aunt Amelia Visits the Zoo

Aunt Amelia kept a journal of all the animals she saw by writing down an anagram of each. Can you decipher her list?

Example: CAROB C O B R A

1. BRAZE   _ZEBRA_
2. FLOW   _WOLF_
3. POPISH   _HIPPOS_
4. TORTE   _OTTER_
5. PAROLED   _LEOPARD_
6. COOLEST   _OCELOTS_
7. CORONA   _RACOON_
8. MANIAC   _____
9. ROOTIEST   _TORTOISE_
10. OOCYTE   _COYOTE_

Zoologist Level

11. PATINA   _____
12. AMASSING _____

Aunt Amelia Visits the Dog Show

Aunt Amelia kept a journal of all the dogs she saw by creating an anagram of each one. Can you decipher her list?

Example: RETAG DEAN   G R E A T   D A N E

1. SPOOLED   _____

2. ORGIC   _____

3. PROTEIN   _____

4. RISHI RETIRER   _____ _____

5. PAINLESS   _____

6. SATIN BRANDER

   _____ _____

7. SOMEDAY   _____

8. BEASTS UNSHOD

   _____ _____

9. SHINGLE TESTERS

   _____ _____

10. LARBOARD   _____

Aunt Amelia Visits the Aviary

Aunt Amelia kept a journal of all the birds she saw by creating an anagram of each one. Can you decipher her list?

Example: ROGUES <u>G R O U S E</u>

1. RENT _____

2. GREET _____

3. HONER _____

4. MISPAGE _____

5. CORDON _____

6. EPIGON _____

7. BRAWLER _____

8. PANICLE _____

9. HOEDOWN _____

10. HORMONE _____

Ornithologist Level

11. TIME-OUTS _____

12. BROKAGES _____

Aunt Amelia Visits the Aquarium

Aunt Amelia kept a journal of all the creatures she saw by creating an anagram of each one. Can you decipher her list?

Example: TUTOR   <u>T R O U T</u>

1. CALM   _____
2. STOREY   _____
3. AUNT   _____
4. HARKS   _____
5. GULLIBLE   _____
6. SANDIER   _____
7. BOLSTER   _____
8. FISHBOWL   _____
9. UNFOLDER   _____
10. STRAYING   _____
11. BALANCER   _____
12. EMANATE   _____
13. SUMLESS   _____

Aunt Amelia Visits the
Botanic Garden

Aunt Amelia kept a journal of all flowers she saw by creating an anagram of each one. Can you decipher her list?

Example: PROMISER   P R I M R O S E

1. TEARS   _____

2. SAYID   _____

3. MUSED   _____

4. AVAILS   _____

5. LINEUP   _____

6. OCCURS   _____

7. SUPINATE   _____

8. RELOANED   _____

9. MEASURING   _____

10. CLIMATES   _____

11. TERMLY   _____

Green Thumb Level

12. STABILE   _____

13. FAERIES   _____

• Trivia •

Litmus Test

Uncle Sylvester, after listening to too many U.S. Senate hearings, became infatuated with the litmus test. He asks you to identify these literary references which contain "mus." He's no ignoramus!

1. Associated with rabbit tales

   — — — — —   — — — — —

2. French author of *The Stranger*

   — — — — — —   — — — — —

3. *La Bohème* character — — — — — — —

4. Dumas swashbuckler — — — — — — — — —

5. "Dublin Fair City" comestible — — — — — — — —

6. Chaplin trademark — — — — — — — —

7. Greek god of censure and mockery — — — — —

8. Private-eye moniker — — — — — —

9. American art form, evolved from vaudeville

   — — — — — — —

10. Alice ate this — — — — — — — —

11. Nine inspiring Greek ladies — — — — —

12. Frenchman (1503–1556) known for his predictions

    — — — — — — — — — —

Lit Test

Many characters in literature, myth, and biblical history are drawn in such a lively way that they have entered our language as nouns and adjectives descriptive of types and classes of people. Test your literary I.Q. with this quiz.

1. From Jonathan Swift's land of little people, used to describe a diminutive or petty person. _____ (adjective)

2. From an American folktale, used to describe someone or something very large. _____ (adjective)

3. Any young woman who comes into good fortune after a period of adversity, from a classic fairy tale. _____ (noun)

4. From the New Testament, one who betrays another under the guise of friendship. _____ (noun)

5. From the Roman god of wine, now used to describe a drunken or carousing person or event. _____ (adjective)

6. A person of extraordinary strength or agility, from Edgar Rice Burroughs hero. _____ (noun)

7. From Dickens, a person who instructs another in crime. _____ (noun)

8. A lament, tale of woe, or complaint, from Old Testament prophet. _____ (noun)

9. A bold and scheming woman, from biblical wife of Ahab. _____ (noun)

• Trivia Anagrams •

What's in a Name?

Creating an anagram from the letters in a celebrity's name sometimes forms interesting phrases vaguely related to the person's attributes, circumstances, role, or occupation. Unscramble each phrase below to discover these famous people—past and present.

Example: LO, HIP SEÑORA   S o p h i a   L o r e n

1. DO BE IN TERROR

    — — — — —   — — — — — —

2. FILLY LEADS __ __ __ __ __   __ __ __ __ __

3. HATED FOR ILL

    — — — — —   — — — — — —

4. DESERVE TO WIN

    — — — — — —   — — — — — —

5. I MAIL ESTROGEN

    — — — — — —   — — — — — — —

6. PAY FOR WHINER

    — — — — —   — — — — — — —

7. ENTREATS VIM __ __ __ __ __   __ __ __ __ __ __

8. SO, I ACT; LED TOWN

    — — — —   — — — — — — — —

9. OH, HAD LINEUP __ __ __ __   __ __ __ __ __ __ __

What's in a Name II?

Know the Write People

Creating an anagram from the letters in a celebrity's name sometimes forms interesting phrases vaguely related to the person's attributes, circumstances or a character or work they have created. Unscramble each phrase below to discover the well-known, not necessarily contemporary, author.

1. A MANLIER NORM

   — — — — —   — — — — — —

2. A LONE PALE DREG

   — — — — —   — — — — —   — —

3. SEE AWRY MEN THING

   — — — — —   — — — — — — — —

4. RAD CLUES IN THORO YARN — — —

   — — — — —   — — — — —   — — — — —

5. I'M SICKLY, DONE IN

   — — — —   — — — — — — —

6. HAD ONE HARDY VIRTUE — — — — —

   — — — — —   — — — — — —

7. ALIENIST MEWLS SEEN

   — — — — — — —   — — — — — — —

8. AH, AIRTIGHT CASE

   — — — — — —   — — — — — —

9. HANDWROTE HIT

   — — — — —   — — — — — —

Global Power

Anagram each word below to find the name of a country—past or present.

Example: PENAL   <u>N e p a l</u>

1. PURE   _____

2. RAIN   _____

3. REIGN   _____

4. RUMBA   _____

5. BIALY   _____

6. LAITY   _____

7. ERECT   _____

8. PINAS   _____

9. ENEMY   _____

10. SAILER   _____

11. ASPIRE   _____

12. ANALOG   _____

13. REGALIA   _____

14. INLACED   _____

15. PENALTIES   _____

Bonus: Many country names are also uncapitalized words with other meanings, for example, *China*. How many country names that are also acceptable words can you find? Compare your answers with our list of sixteen. Ten is a super score!

Global Power II

Anagram each word below to find the name of large cities in different parts of the world.

Example: PANELS   N a p l e s, Italy

1. SALVAGES   _ _ _   _ _ _ _ _

2. INWARD   _ _ _ _ _ _

3. UNITS   _ _ _ _ _

4. EVINCE   _ _ _ _ _ _

5. GOALS   _ _ _ _ _

6. DOTTIER   _ _ _ _ _ _ _

7. HASTEN   _ _ _ _ _ _

8. VALIANCE   _ _ _ _ _ _ _ _

9. LOUSE   _ _ _ _ _

10. DELES   _ _ _ _ _

11. DIAGNOSE   _ _ _   _ _ _ _ _

12. SAUNAS   _ _ _ _ _ _

13. COUNTS   _ _ _ _ _ _

14. CASCARA   _ _ _ _ _ _ _

15. GASOLENES   _ _ _   _ _ _ _ _ _

Global Power III

Anagram each set of letters below to find the name of large cities in different parts of the world. Believe it or not, each of these cities is also an acceptable word with another meaning.

Example: A A C E G H N O R   A n c h o r a g e, Alaska, U.S.A.

1. AADMRS   _____

2. ABHT   _____

3. DELOOT   _____

4. ABFFLOU   _____

5. AIPRS   _____

6. AARSWW   _____

7. CDEEINOPRV   _____

8. EHINOPX   _____

9. AAILMN   _____

10. ABGHMRU   _____

11. ABDEORUX   _____

12. ACIIORTV   _____

• Anagrams •

Symbolically Speaking

:   .   *   +   %   ]   ,   /

Use *one* of the symbols above as a base word along with the extra letters designated, to discover the word indicated in the clue.

Example: __ and P = movie featuring a mermaid
__/__ (SLASH) and P = <u>Splash</u>

1. __ and V = to furnish or supply

2. __ and Y = a territory settled in a distant land

3. __ and E = rhythmic pattern of heartbeat tested at wrist

4. __ and M = those who misunderstand

5. __ and S = a support for the spinal area

6. __ and R = to eat or drink in a noisy manner

7. __ and U = not very hip

8. __ and H K = a nice place to spend a summer afternoon

9. __ and B I = one who speaks spitefully or slanderously about another person

10. __ and A V = Stromboli, for one

11. __ and E J = some drinks popular in the southern U.S.

Want Adz from A to Z

Each of these twenty-six words is an anagram for a single word, and each answer starts with a different letter of the alphabet. Use the chart below to keep track of the initial letter of each anagram.

1. FINKED _____
2. MINGLER _____
3. GROUTY _____
4. RAGWEED _____
5. TRAVEL _____
6. TEETHES _____
7. DEMISED _____
8. BRAILLE _____
9. TABLET _____
10. SIX _____
11. UNPOSTED _____
12. DOZEN _____
13. APLENTY _____

14. MANTRAP _____
15. IRKSOME _____
16. LIMPED _____
17. SMARTER _____
18. MUNDANE _____
19. LOUDEN _____
20. INFESTS _____
21. PATCHES _____
22. GYRATED _____
23. SOUPÇON _____
24. TRIJET _____
25. TENSION _____
26. REQUIRE _____

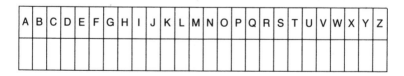

A	B	C	D	E	F	G	H	I	J	K	L	M	N	O	P	Q	R	S	T	U	V	W	X	Y	Z

Want Adz II, Short List

Each of these words is an anagram and has only one solution. Each starts with a different letter of the alphabet. Use the chart below to keep track of the initial letter of each anagram.

1. INFLATOR _____
2. SIMPLEST _____
3. ROASTING _____
4. NOBLESSE _____
5. RIVALING _____
6. SPECTRUM _____
7. CAVIARE _____
8. MINUTELY _____
9. REVOLUTE _____
10. METERING _____
11. REQUITAL _____
12. MONODIES _____
13. POUCHIER _____
14. DRAINAGE _____
15. DESPITES _____
16. RAPIDER _____
17. CHESTIER _____
18. MISWROTE _____
19. TIDINESS _____
20. RETITLED _____
21. TREATY _____
22. INCENSES _____

A	B	C	D	E	F	G	H	I	J	K	L	M	N	O	P	Q	R	S	T	U	V	W	X	Y	Z

Want Adz III, Short List

Each of these words is an anagram and has only one solution. Each starts with a different letter of the alphabet. Use the chart below to keep track of the initial letter of each anagram.

1. DEMURRER _____
2. ROSEOLA _____
3. MONEYBAG _____
4. OUTCURSE _____
5. NATIVISM _____
6. SQUATTER _____
7. TOPSOIL _____
8. PROPOSE _____
9. PIMENTOS _____
10. DOWERIES _____
11. DRAYMEN _____
12. SHARING _____
13. STEEPLED _____
14. MUTILATE _____
15. REFINING _____
16. INTERRED _____
17. DISPLODE _____
18. MOONIEST _____
19. EPITAPHS _____
20. UNDERFED _____
21. FINISHED _____
22. HUSTLING _____

A	B	C	D	E	F	G	H	I	J	K	L	M	N	O	P	Q	R	S	T	U	V	W	X	Y	Z

Dog Catcher

Keeping the order given, add the letters D O G (not necessarily in that order) to the strings of letters below to catch some common words.

Example: R A N S N   <u>GranDsOn</u>

1. I R L H O
2. E V U R I N
3. K N W L E E
4. R U N H O G
5. W N R A D E
6. W R N O E R
7. R A N F L Y
8. E X P L I N
9. V A A B N
10. S H A W I N
11. L E N R O D
12. C N E S T E

13. R A I O L Y
14. B A N W A N
15. M R T A G E
16. B L I A T E
17. U I E B O K
18. U N E R N E
19. R A N E A E
20. H Y R E N
21. H E A L N
22. M A R I L
23. I A N S I S
24. P R I I E S

Manhunt

Keeping the order given, add the letters M A N (not necessarily in that order) to the strings of letters below to discover the common words hidden in this MANHUNT.

Example: A R T H O   <u>MarAthoN</u>

<table>
<tr><td>1. B D O I A L</td><td>13. B E C H R K</td></tr>
<tr><td>2. I G I A R Y</td><td>14. A B O R L</td></tr>
<tr><td>3. C A R O I</td><td>15. S C R A E T</td></tr>
<tr><td>4. L E B R A I</td><td>16. C I E T I C</td></tr>
<tr><td>5. L I G A N T</td><td>17. D O I N C E</td></tr>
<tr><td>6. D Y I T E</td><td>18. G E R I U</td></tr>
<tr><td>7. I P T I E T</td><td>19. C H I E R Y</td></tr>
<tr><td>8. F L I G O</td><td>20. R I S T O R</td></tr>
<tr><td>9. I P O R T T</td><td>21. E O P U S E</td></tr>
<tr><td>10. G R O P H O E</td><td>22. G E T I C</td></tr>
<tr><td>11. S P E R I T</td><td>23. C O E D I</td></tr>
<tr><td>12. E O T I O L</td><td>24. E U E R T E</td></tr>
</table>

• Category Puzzles •

Joint Custody

Find the one word that combines, in front or back, with each word in each set below to form a phrase, name, title, or compound word.

Example: SHOT, BLUE, THIRSTY, MOBILE <u>blood</u>
BLOODshot, blueBLOOD, BLOODthirsty, BLOODmobile

1. REAR, PICTURE, DRESSING, WASHER

2. DOG, WHITE, DRESS, HOLD

3. CASTLE, STORM, BAG, MAN

4. TALKS, BAG, MARKET, FUNNY

5. MEAL, KNOT, DANCE, ROOT

6. ROSE, WHACK, LEAGUE, GEORGE

7. ORGAN, PEACE, DOWN, DREAM

8. DUST, BROWN, GHOST, CRABBE

9. PARADISE, CAP, GOLD, ERRAND

10. FAITH, DATE, SPOT, DUCK

Joint Custody II

Find the one word that combines, in front or back, with each word in each set below to form a phrase, name, title, or compound word.

Example: HALL, TAP, SQUARE, OF DEATH <u>dance</u>
DANCE hall, tap DANCE, square DANCE, DANCE of death

1. MARKET, DOG, DOZER, PAPAL

2. COPY, NIP, TAIL, WALK

3. TAG, CHILI, HANG, UNDER

4. HOUSE, EYED, LITTER, DOODLE

5. VIRGIN, CONTROL, MARK, STONE

6. SHORT, CREW, GLASS, UPPER

7. POSTER, SCORE, H, FLUSHER

8. HOLE, GLOVE, HOUND, FIRE

9. CREAM, HOCKEY, CAP, BREAKER

10. EXPOSURE, HEMISPHERE, IRELAND, LIGHTS

Joint Custody III

Find the one word that combines, in front or back, with each word in each set below to form a phrase, name, title, or compound word.

Example: GUN, BLUE, PUFF, FACE   <u>powder</u>
gun<small>POWDER</small>, <small>POWDER</small> blue, <small>POWDER</small> puff, face <small>POWDER</small>

1. SEA, GAME, SHOCK, FISH

2. CHICKEN, FEVER, BOARD, WATER

3. HEADED, LATIN, PORKY, STY

4. POTION, AFFAIR, SEAT, TRUE

5. CHEST, DIAMOND, LESS, BOB

6. SLIPPER, HOUSES, LOOKING, MENAGERIE

7. SLIDE, EEL, ORGAN, CHAIR

8. HOT, FAMINE, SWEET, CHIP

9. STATES, NATIONS, PRESS INTERNATIONAL, KINGDOM

10. CAR, JACKET, GUN, NO

Joint Custody IV

Find the one word that combines, in front or back, with each word in each set below to form a phrase, name, title, or compound word.

Example: HORSE, FOAM, LEGS, MONSTER   <u>sea</u>
           SEA horse, SEA foam, SEA legs, SEA monster

1. GREEN, NAIL, TACK, SCREW

2. BITE, ROBERT, JACK, HOAR

3. OMELET, SPAGHETTI, FRONT, FRONTIER

4. SAUCER, BUTTRESS, FEAR OF, COLORS

5. BEER, SNAP, ROGERS, BREAD

6. MUFFIN, BODY, LANGUAGE, CHANNEL

7. SILVER, BREAD, FED, TABLE

8. ATTACK, BEAN, CLOCKWISE, ESPIONAGE

9. DRESSING, DOORS, TOAST, FRIES

10. FATHER, BOMB, CAPSULE, IMMEMORIAL

Joint Custody V

Find the one word that combines, in front or back, with each word in each set below to form a phrase, name, title, or compound word.

Example: JOY, UP, BROOM, PIN   <u>stick</u>
joySTICK, STICKup, broomSTICK, STICKpin

1. RADISH, POWER, SHOE, SENSE

2. ABOUT, LIFT, TYPE, BOLD

3. GUESS, STRING, CHILDHOOD, NATURE

4. ROAD, BOAT, BUSINESS, PLACE

5. TUBE, CITY, SANCTUM, DIRECTED

6. DELIGHT, TOWEL, BATH, EMPIRE

7. BRICK, BOY, VAMPIRE, DING

8. SUPREME, JESTER, HOUSE, MARTIAL

9. BORN, SPIRIT, LANCE, GERM

10. BROTHER, THE SUNDANCE, GLOVES, SKIN

Common Denominator

Divide the list of items below into five categories of three items each. Use each item just once. Some items may fit into more than one category, but only one solution uses all words.

BANANAS   KERMIT   SOCIETY
CANARY   MANHATTAN TOILET BOWL
CHEESE   MONEY   TOOTH
COFFEE   PAINT   VIRGIN
GRASS   SLEEPER   WEDDING

Category _Things That Are Green_ : <u>grass</u>, _____

and _____.

Category _____ : _____, _____

and _____.

Category _____ : _____, _____

and _____.

Category _____ : _____, _____

and _____.

Category _____ : _____, _____

and _____.

Common Denominator II

Divide the list of names below into five categories of three items each. Use each name just once. Some may fit into more than one category, but only one solution uses all names.

ALLEN	DUDLEY	MARY
CHER	ETHEL	MARY TYLER
DEAN	GUTHRIE	PRINCE
DEMI	LIONEL	STEVE
DREW	MADONNA	WOODPECKER

Category <u>Moores</u> : <u>Demi</u>, _____

and _____.

Category _____ : _____, _____

and _____.

Category _____ : _____, _____

and _____.

Category _____ : _____, _____

and _____.

Category _____ : _____, _____

and _____.

Common Denominator III

Divide the list of items below into five categories of three items each. Use each item just once. Some items may fit into more than one category, but only one solution uses all words.

FLINT   DEAD BODY   PEANUTS
JERK   FROST   GALL
GINGER   ROLLING   SARSAPARILLA
BURNS   JACK   PONY
FLARE   BROWNING   MASHED
                              POTATO

Category Stones : Rolling, _____

and _____.

Category _____ : _____, _____

and _____.

Category _____ : _____, _____

and _____.

Category _____ : _____, _____

and _____.

Category _____ : _____, _____

and _____.

Common Denominator IV

Divide the list of items below into five categories of three items each. Use each item just once. Some items may fit into more than one category, but only one solution uses all words.

GUITAR   IPANEMA   JULIA
MIAMI   SUNFLOWER   TRAIN
COTTON   COLD   OMAHA
FEVER   RITA   COWARD
FISH   NOSE   MICHELLE

Category   "Yellow" Things :   sunflower, _____

and _____.

Category _____ : _____, _____

and _____.

Category _____ : _____, _____

and _____.

Category _____ : _____, _____

and _____.

Category _____ : _____, _____

and _____.

Common Denominator V

Divide the list of items below into five categories of three items each. Use each item just once. Some items may fit into more than one category, but only one solution uses all words.

BALANCHINE   ANNE   POMPIDOU
SIMON   RAY CHARLES   JOHN
EMILY   ROUND   HELEN KELLER
OEDIPUS REX   THOMAS   FLANK
CHUCK   HARRISON   CHARLOTTE

Category _Brontë Sisters_ : _Emily,_ _____

and _____.

Category _____ : _____, _____

and _____.

Category _____ : _____, _____

and _____.

Category _____ : _____, _____

and _____.

Category _____ : _____, _____

and _____.

Common Denominator VI

Divide the list of items below into five categories of three items each. Use each item just once. Some items may fit into more than one category, but only one solution uses all words.

BLOOD PRESSURE   KISS   BUBBLE
AIR   JUNK   ZIPPER
CANYON   MARRIAGE   SLAM
POETIC   PIANO   REGISTERED
NOSE   DOG   ELEVATOR

Category Things That Go Up :   elevator, _____

and _____.

Category _____ : _____, _____

and _____.

Category _____ : _____, _____

and _____.

Category _____ : _____, _____

and _____.

Category _____ : _____, _____

and _____.

• Letter Patterns •

Angelic Devilry

Insert all the letters, not necessarily in order, from the word ANGEL or DEVIL in the blanks below to form acceptable words.

Example: C O N G E N I A L
           C I V I L I Z E D

1. J _ _ _ _ _

2. _ E _ _ R _ _

3. _ O _ _ B _ R _

4. _ _ _ _ C _

5. _ _ S S O _ _ _

6. _ _ _ U _ G _ D

7. _ A S _ _ _ _

8. _ A N _ A _ _ Z _

9. A _ O _ _ A B _ _

10. H _ _ O _ _ _

11. _ E _ _ _ _

12. _ _ S O _ I _ _

13. _ R _ _ _ _

14. _ I _ _ _ _ E

15. _ _ _ _ _ _ O E R

16. F I _ _ _ _ _ D

17. _ _ _ I _ _

18. _ _ _ R _ I _ S T

Guys & Gals

Insert all the letters, not necessarily in order, from the word GUY or GAL in the blanks below to form acceptable words.

Example: H U <u>R</u> R <u>Y</u> I N <u>G</u>
          H O <u>L</u> O <u>G</u> R <u>A</u> M

1. _ _ I L T _   10. _ _ U _ H T E R

2. F L _ _ P O _ E   11. _ A _ Z _

3. B O D _ _ _ A R D   12. S _ _ A R _

4. T _ N _ E _ O   13. _ O _ _ R T

5. S I N _ U _ _ R   14. L A D _ B _ _

6. B U R _ _ N D _   15. E _ E _ _ N T

7. S _ N A _ O G _ E   16. N E _ R O L O _ _

8. _ O _ N _   17. H O O _ I _ _ N

9. H _ N _ N A I _   18. _ _ R N E _

Twofers

Use all the letters from one of the two words (such as *award* or *night* in the first set) below, not necessarily in the order given, to fill in the blanks and decipher hidden words. These puzzles use common words, but being aware of common prefixes, suffixes, and word patterns will help you.

Answers to Challenge questions may be proper names. They do not necessarily draw on letters from these key words.

Award Night

Example: A N Y <u>t</u> <u>h</u> <u>i</u> <u>n</u> <u>g</u>   H a R d w a r E

1. __ W K __ __ __ __ L Y
2. __ U __ __ R __ E S __
3. L E __ __ __ __ __ E R
4. W __ I S __ L __ __ __
5. B O __ __ __ __ __ L K

6. H __ __ D S I __ __ __
7. __ __ S H B O __ __ __
8. __ R __ O __ H E __ __
9. __ F T E R __ __ __ __
10. G U __ F __ __ __ __

Challenge: What is the highest U.S. award (perhaps comparable to the Academy Award) given for achievement in advertising?

Coca-Cola (Coca and Cola)

Example: a c c o R D I O N   D I P l o M a c Y

1. __ L __ __ H O L I __
2. B __ __ H E __ __ R
3. I L __ __ G I __ __ L

4. S T __ __ K __ __ R
5. C __ __ K R O __ __ H
6. W __ S H __ __ __ __ T H

94

7. D E M __ __ R __ __ Y   9. __ R __ S S W __ __ K

8. S __ __ R E __ __ R D   10. __ __ A T R __ __ K

Challenge: What parts of the cola tree yield the extract used in the manufacture of cola drinks?

Moby Dick

Example: m o N E y b A G   G R i d L O c k

1. T __ __ __ O __   6. H __ __ N __ __ O K

2. B A __ __ S __ __ E   7. S __ __ E K I __ __

3. __ U __ __ L __ N G   8. B __ __ __ E R E __

4. H __ __ E __ O D __   9. S __ __ __ __ L I C

5. H A N __ P __ __ __   10. W __ __ __ E __ L Y

Challenge: What is the famous sentence which begins Herman Melville's classic novel *Moby Dick*?

Santa Claus

Example: F a n a t I C s   c a l C U L u s

1. __ __ __ __ Z __   6. __ O __ __ __ L G I __

2. __ G __ I __ __ __   7. __ P __ __ __ __ E

3. M __ __ I __ __ __   8. M __ __ __ __ __ I N E

4. __ __ __ L Y __ __   9. P H E __ __ __ __ __

5. __ __ __ __ A __   10. __ __ __ G E H __ __ D

Challenge: What country owns Christmas Island?

Talk Show

Example: w <u>o</u> R <u>s</u> h I P   t H <u>a</u> N <u>k</u> F U <u>l</u>

1. C O C __ __ __ I __
2. __ E A __ R T __ Y
3. B __ __ N __ E __ E D
4. __ __ N E Y D E __ __
5. __ I __ __ B __ N E

6. __ E __ __ E T T __ E
7. __ __ __ L E __ A L E
8. T __ __ N __ __ I P
9. W __ __ __ A __ H O N
10. F O __ __ __ __ L E

Challenge: If guests talk about a klieg light, is the talk show about medicine, near-death experiences, or movie-making?

Babe Ruth

Example: b <u>a</u> R <u>b</u> e R   t r O <u>u</u> G <u>h</u>

1. A __ __ __ O __
2. __ __ __ __ S T
3. __ __ __ __ Y
4. __ A I __ C __ __
5. __ __ R __ __ L L

6. B __ __ C __ E __
7. __ A R __ __ __ C K
8. C __ __ __ C __
9. F O __ __ __ __
10. __ __ A N __ __ G

Challenge: Who starred as Babe Ruth in the movie *Babe*?

Hot Dog

Example: M <u>o</u> N <u>t</u> <u>h</u> L Y   K I N <u>g</u> <u>d</u> <u>o</u> M

1. B __ __ __
2. __ __ U R __

3. __ __ __ U
4. __ I S __ __ R I C

5. P _ _ _ O   8. C _ O C _ L A _ E

6. I N _ I _ _   9. P A _ _ _ A

7. _ U M _ R _ P   10. _ E R E _ _

Challenge: If you're *hotdogging*, what are you doing?

Round Table

Example: S Q u A d r o n   l U b R I C a t e

1. G _ E Y H _ _ _ _   6. _ A _ G E _ _ _ S

2. _ _ P H A _ _ _   7. V E R I _ _ _ _ _

3. A _ J _ _ _ _ E D   8. C E _ E _ R _ _ _

4. I _ T _ _ _ _ C E   9. M _ A _ _ _ _ L

5. _ _ _ _ I S H E _   10. S C _ _ _ _ _ E L

Challenge: Dorothy Parker, James Thurber, and other literary giants met at a round table in what famous New York hotel?

Crew Neck

Example: c O O K w A r e   D e c k H A n D

1. _ _ _ _ K   6. R _ _ _ O _

2. _ I T _ H _ _   7. N I _ _ _ A M _

3. M I _ _ O _ A V _   8. _ A _ T _ H _ E L

4. _ S _ _ O _   9. _ U _ F _ _

5. H _ _ P E _ _   10. _ O _ _ I T _

Challenge: What 1940s movie star was known as the "sweater girl"?

Mom, Dad

Example: B A L <u>d</u> H E <u>a</u> <u>d</u>   A m <u>m</u> <u>o</u> N I A

1. A _ _ _   6. _ I _ E _
2. _ _ D E _   7. _ _ F F O _ I L
3. _ A _ B _   8. C O _ _ A N D _
4. C _ _ _ A   9. S Y _ P T _ _
5. _ E C _ _ E   10. _ _ N _ E L I O N

Challenge: The word *parents* has four anagrams. How many can you find?

Soul Mate

Example: A B <u>s</u> <u>o</u> <u>l</u> <u>u</u> T E   <u>a</u> N <u>t</u> <u>e</u> R O O <u>m</u>

1. H I _ A R I _ _ _   6. D _ _ I _ _ S S E
2. C A R _ _ _ E _   7. N I G H _ _ _ R _
3. H _ _ R G _ A S _   8. M _ _ K M E _ _ N
4. D _ _ D R _ M _   9. G H _ _ _ I _ H
5. B _ S _ _ E N _   10. B _ R O _ _ _ E R

Challenge: In Greek myth, who was the sculpted soul mate of Pygmalion, brought to life by Aphrodite?

Onion Field

Example: W i <u>l</u> <u>d</u> L I <u>f</u> <u>e</u>   S n <u>o</u> <u>o</u> Z i <u>n</u> G

1. _ _ _ C K _ R E _   3. _ P I _ _ _ _ A T E D
2. M _ _ _ S H _ _ E   4. _ _ _ _ _ G U A R _

98

5. _ R O _ _ C K _ _   8. C _ _ T _ _ U _ US

6. C _ M M U _ _ _ _   9. _ _ _ T _ X _ C

7. Q U A _ I _ _ _ _   10. C _ M P A _ _ _ _

Challenge: Who is the author of the novel *The Onion Field*, based on a true event, made into a film?

Zig, Zag

Example: g <u>a</u> R B A N <u>z</u> O   E N E R <u>g</u> <u>i</u> <u>z</u> E

1. _ _ _ M O   6. O R _ A N _ _

2. O O _ _ N _   7. S T _ R _ A _ E R

3. M A _ _ _ I N E   8. _ O O L O _ _ S T

4. _ _ _ E B O   9. _ _ _ E L L E

5. _ L _ T _   10. C O _ N I _ _ N T

Challenge: Elias Howe invented the sewing machine in what year: 1824, 1846, 1865, or 1887?

Army, Navy

Example: F <u>a</u> <u>r</u> <u>m</u> <u>y</u> A R D   H E <u>a</u> <u>v</u> E <u>n</u> L <u>y</u>

1. _ _ _ O R _   6. _ N _ _ O _ E

2. _ I L I T _ _ _   7. S _ _ _ T _

3. _ _ R _ I _ G   8. _ O L U _ T _ R _

4. _ _ J O _ I T _   9. P H _ _ _ _ A C _

5. _ _ C H O _ _   10. _ I _ E _ _ R D

Challenge: Where are the U.S. Naval Academy and the U.S. Military Academy located?

Milan, Italy

Example: C O m P l a i n   a B i l I t y

1. _ _ U _ _ _   6. A _ _ _ _ _
2. _ _ _ _ N _   7. _ _ B _ R _ N _ H
3. _ _ X _ _ _   8. _ O _ O R _ _ _
4. _ _ _ _ _ Y   9. P O _ _ C E _ _ _
5. _ _ P _ C _ _   10. D _ _ _ _ G H _

Challenge: What is the Italian name for the city of Milan?

Far Out

Example: a I r f A R E   A S t o u N D

1. D W _ _ _ _   6. B _ R R I _ _
2. _ _ _ P I A   7. S T _ _ _ I S H
3. _ _ F _   8. M _ _ S E _ R A P
4. _ _ B _ I C   9. E _ _ _ U L
5. D _ _ B _   10. _ _ G B _ A T

Challenge: What "far out" Beat Generation poet authored the landmark poem "Howl"?

Shin Bone

Example: A s T O n i S h   b o O K e n D

1. _ A _ D W _ C _   4. A _ D _ M _ _
2. _ _ X T E E _ T _   5. R E _ _ L L I _ _
3. D _ _ _ _ A I R   6. H O M _ _ _ _ U _ D

7. C _ R _ _ T E _   9. C U _ _ _ _ O _ E D

8. W _ R K _ _ _ _ E C H   10. _ Y P _ O T _ _ T

Challenge: What is the scientific name for the shin bone?

Fish Soup

Example: <u>s</u> <u>o</u> A <u>p</u> S <u>u</u> D S   <u>h</u> O U <u>s</u> E W <u>i</u> f E

1. _ L O U R _ _ _   6. _ _ O P L _ _ T

2. H _ M E _ _ _ N   7. _ _ R _ T _ A N D

3. _ C _ L _ T _ R   8. C _ _ R T _ H I _

4. _ _ R E _ O U _ E   9. _ _ A C I _ _ S

5. A _ T _ _ _ Y   10. _ _ I S O N O _ _

Challenge: What is the name of the popular French fish soup made in Provence?

Toy Box

Example: A U <u>t</u> H <u>o</u> R I T <u>y</u>   <u>b</u> <u>o</u> R D E A U <u>x</u>

1. A T _ _ R N E _   6. B _ D _ S U I _

2. G E _ M E _ R _   7. E _ H I _ I T _ R

3. _ _ _ L O O D   8. M A _ R I M _ N _

4. _ _ P H _ O N   9. T E _ T _ _ O K

5. L A V A _ _ R _   10. O _ N O _ I _ U S

Challenge: From these anagrams, find "toy box" classics: STEAKS, BROAD MAGES, BLAMERS.

Fast Food

Example: f A N T a s t I C   D R I f T W o o d

1. W _ _ _ E _ U L

2. _ _ I N T E _ _

3. _ I R E W _ _ _

4. M _ _ _ E R _ U L

5. _ _ N _ A _ I Z E

6. P R _ _ _ E _

7. B E E _ _ _ E _ K

8. C _ M _ _ R T E _

9. C _ N _ _ U N _ E R

10. _ L _ _ _ G A T E

Challenge: The anagram LONGED CHASER represents the symbol of what fast food chain?

• Answers •

Word Structure

"X" Marks the Spot

1. buxom
2. Fix-It
3. moxie
4. boxer (Joe Louis)
5. Texas
6. pixie
7. dioxide
8. Quixote
9. inexact
10. proxies
11. prexies, Marxists
12. nonexpert
13. peroxides
14. obnoxious
15. faxes
16. maxim
17. mix-up

Split Ends

1. presto
2. laxest
3. aboard
4. notice
5. chorale
6. bureau
7. baleen
8. lament
9. opined
10. poverty
11. thorny
12. flowery
13. upland
14. frugal
15. timider
16. filial
17. cheapo
18. funded
19. fabric
20. gundog
21. chide
22. dryad
23. among
24. hyena
25. ovate
26. turbo
27. cacti
28. abate
29. welsh
30. afire

Split Ends II

1. greedy
2. bravery
3. widest
4. neuron
5. awoken
6. equated
7. awhirl
8. renown
9. change
10. nonuse
11. disbar
12. croquet
13. evilly
14. limpid
15. oration
16. tragic
17. please
18. unopen
19. finial
20. wintery
21. apart
22. emote
23. leggy
24. ivied
25. mirky
26. hadst
27. apish
28. djinn
29. moldy
30. veldt

Split Ends III

1. apron
2. known
3. ovary
4. exist
5. adieu
6. whipt
7. amuse
8. milky
9. globe
10. twist
11. ajuga
12. awash
13. eking
14. burnt
15. gnawn
16. rinse
17. theme
18. flaxy
19. aging
20. acute
21. chosen
22. yeasty
23. lacrosse
24. chesty
25. climax
26. lattice
27. educate
28. bleary
29. windiest
30. cranky

Split Ends Plus

1. shiest	9. screwy	17. shiver	25. salient
2. skiddoo	10. stingless	18. stardom	26. scumming
3. sexpot	11. scribe	19. jauntier	27. flamingo
4. fogless	12. scampi	20. sharpy	28. scowl
5. scrawl	13. sparest	21. ethyl	29. checkless
6. stalkier	14. smarty	22. safari	30. achiness
7. slobbery	15. sexiness	23. playa	
8. braless	16. sheath	24. snipe	

Expansion Joint

1. bodices	9. habitant	17. turnkey	25. depreciate
2. imperial	10. hideouts	18. excerpt	26. contingent
3. rotund	11. imprudent	19. gonad	27. nutriment
4. falsie	12. bedside	20. mortality	28. insolvent
5. monody	13. playday	21. baluster	29. antitrust
6. gentile	14. curious	22. cowshed	30. freshmen
7. cornmeal	15. belated	23. waterbed	
8. monkeyed	16. mousse	24. expiration	

Whodunit

1. J nonparty	7. L schmooze	13. K printout
2. N trueblue	8. O unafraid	14. B boroughs
3. H jaundice	9. I maharaja	15. Q whodunit
4. P weevilly	10. D crossway	16. C caravans
5. E earplugs	11. F ghettoed	17. M shrewish
6. G harbours	12. A barstool	

Whodunit II

1. A alphabet	7. K pinafore	13. E episodes
2. Q whizbang	8. D doorjamb	14. J pastrami
3. O seascape	9. I lockjaws	15. P wheatear
4. F fiancées	10. B antimale	16. N scrutiny
5. G icebergs	11. H inhumane	17. C blastoff
6. M reviewer	12. L quagmire	

Whodunit III

1. F nondairy	7. A benefits	13. D flyspeck
2. K rockabye	8. G nosegays	14. N theorems
3. E minibike	9. O tomahawk	15. B crosscut
4. Q vagabond	10. M shellacs	16. P trusteed
5. J pushcart	11. C dominoes	17. L sandwich
6. H pacifist	12. I peignoir	

Whodunit IV

1. C emblazon	7. A armchair	13. Q thespian
2. E jailbait	8. K sapphire	14. F monopoly
3. B disobeys	9. P teashops	15. I reattach
4. M standoff	10. G outblaze	16. H plastics
5. L sauterne	11. O subunits	17. J salivary
6. N stargaze	12. D ensconce	

Whodunit V

1. C barmaids	7. O residual	13. D chaplain
2. E cochairs	8. M plaudits	14. L lovelily
3. H flabbier	9. G druggist	15. P sycamore
4. K halibuts	10. N ranchero	16. B asterisk
5. J glaucoma	11. F cousinly	17. I frosteds
6. A albacore	12. Q whiskeys	

eYESight

1. naPOLEon	5. sHANGhai	9. aPARTheid	13. uTENsil
2. oDOMEter	6. banKNOTe	10. poINSETtia	14. epsILOn
3. keROSEne	7. meRINGue	11. iTINErary	15. patRIOTic
4. bACHElor	8. gRAFFiti	12. masTERMind	

eYESight II

1. piMIENto	5. arcHANGel	9. mosQUITo	13. criTICism
2. heREINto	6. proPAGANda	10. comFORTer	14. aSPARagus
3. pROSEcute	7. cLOVERleaf	11. impROMPtu	15. alcOHOlic
4. memBRANe	8. sTILEtto	12. afTERMath	

eYESight III
1. itCHINess
2. orCHEStra
3. marsHALEd
4. dySENTery
5. antiPASTO
6. milLIONth
7. paRAPEts
8. bLOCKade
9. pHARMacy
10. cHAIRman
11. asCRIBes
12. pLATEau
13. ameTHYst
14. bROWnies
15. hoUSEboy

eYESight IV
1. sNOWsuit
2. maCARoni
3. cARMaker
4. doWNbeat
5. impRUDEnt
6. misTHINk
7. nePOTism
8. miNUTest
9. gunFIGht
10. toPOLOgy
11. tiNINEss
12. superHERO
13. cLIENtele
14. taBLEWare
15. unSTABle

Expert eYESight
1. misCONCEption
2. parTICiple
3. thUNDERclap
4. cenTIMEter
5. cANTIlever
6. hoUSEwife
7. conDENSate
8. carboHYDRAte
9. bomBARDier
10. aPOSTrophe
11. proLIFErate
12. maTHEMATICian

Puns & Anagrams

Joyce Shtick—Hospital
1. ambulance: anagram of male Cuban
2. I.C.U.: I see you
3. surgery: Sir + anagram of grey
4. gurney: anagram of un-grey
5. intern: in turn
6. admission: A "D," miss, I only
7. X-ray room: X [after W] + ray + room
8. maternity: anagram of may I rent this
9. emergency: anagram of Gene + mercy
10. insurance: anagram of I can sue, R.N.

Joyce Shtick—Paris
1. Seine: <u>sane</u>
2. Champs-Elysees: anagram of <u>cheesy</u> + <u>samples</u>
3. Orly: anagram of <u>royally</u> minus <u>lay</u>
4. Louvre: anagram of <u>velour</u>
5. Tuileries: anagram of <u>it</u> + <u>leisure</u>
6. Metro: ti<u>me trouble</u>?
7. Notre Dame: <u>not red, A meander</u>
8. Mona Lisa: anagram of <u>so</u> + <u>animal</u>
9. Napoleon: anagram of <u>noon</u> + <u>leap</u>
10. Versailles: <u>over, sail less</u>
11. Latin Quarter: <u>Quartarius</u> (Latin for "quarter")

Joyce Shtick—High School
1. computer: sit<u>com put Erica</u>
2. exams: anagram of <u>Maxes</u>
3. gym: <u>Jim</u>
4. algebra: anagram of <u>gradable</u> − D
5. midterm: anagram of <u>trimmed</u>
6. art: <u>Art</u>hur
7. English: anagram of <u>shingle</u>
8. Spanish: wing<u>span is helpful</u>
9. assignment: anagram of <u>SN</u> + <u>steaming</u>
10. teacher: anagram of <u>cheater</u>
11. senior: <u>"C" in your</u>
12. chemistry: <u>Sachem is trying</u>

Joyce Shtick—Visiting the Zoo
1. owlet: anagram of <u>towel</u>
2. parrot: anagram of <u>raptor</u>
3. lemur: agi<u>le muralist</u>
4. antelope: <u>aunt elope</u>
5. carnivore: anagram of <u>Veronica</u> + R
6. flamingo: <u>flaming</u> orange?
7. kingsnake: anagram of <u>sneaking</u> + K
8. pheasant: anagram of <u>ten</u> + <u>has</u> + <u>Pa</u>
9. egret: fore<u>leg retains</u>
10. bear: <u>bare</u>
11. caiman: anagram of <u>maniac</u>
12. tortoise: anagram of <u>rootiest</u>
13. forest: Be<u>fore strolling</u>

Joyce Shtick—Joy of Foods
1. rosemary: <u>Rose marry</u>
2. lobster: anagram of <u>bolster</u>
3. sole: <u>soul</u>
4. anchovies: anagram of <u>ha</u> + <u>novices</u>

5. kitchen: anagram of thicken
6. abalone: crab alone
7. liverwurst: deliver worst!
8. meringue: anagram of regimen + u (you)
9. pears: Pairs

10. swordfish: Mary's word, fish
11. hamburger: anagram of bear hug + MR
12. ketchup: catch up
13. artichoke: with art, I choke

Joyce Shtick—A Day at the Office
1. appointment: anagram of Pat + mention + P
2. office: anagram of coiffe
3. system: messy, stemware
4. clinch: cinch + L (50)
5. spreadsheet: anagram of she + predates
6. calendar: practical, end around

7. postage: anagram of gestapo
8. chairmen: anagram of machine + R (are)
9. switch: S + which (witch)
10. document: anagram of counted + M (1,000)
11. write: right

Word Doodles & Alphacryptics

Cooking Class
1. banana split
2. chopped liver
3. scrambled eggs
4. apple turnover
5. prune pudding
6. catsup
7. pheasant under glass
8. pears in port wine
9. leftovers
10. round steak
11. pineapple upside-down cake
12. French bread
13. mixed salad
14. shortbread
15. shrimp cocktail
16. eggs over easy

Songs & Musical Compositions
1. "Stand by Me"
2. "Wind Beneath My Wings"
3. "Unfinished Symphony"
4. "The First Noël"
5. "Tiptoe through the Tulips"
6. "Born in the USA"
7. "Moonlight Sonata"
8. "Bridge over Troubled Waters"
9. "High Hopes"

T.V. Time

1. "Little House on the Prairie"
2. "Cheers"
3. "Wheel of Fortune"
4. "48 Hours"
5. "Upstairs Downstairs"
6. "C.H.I.P.S."
7. "Edge of Night"
8. "Murder, She Wrote"
9. "The Price Is Right"

People

1. Flip Wilson
2. Mae West
3. Shelley Long
4. Tina Turner
5. Tiny Tim
6. John Updike
7. Benny Hill
8. Glenn Close
9. Count Basie

Matinee

1. *West Side Story*
2. *French Connection*
3. *Big Top Pee Wee*
4. *From Here to Eternity*
5. *Stripes*
6. *Lost Weekend*
7. *Willow*
8. *Continental Divide*
9. *High Noon* or *Twelve O'Clock High*

Matinee II

1. *All Quiet on the Western Front*
2. *The Big Sleep*
3. *Dr. Dolittle*
4. *Wholly Moses!*
5. *Gone with the Wind,*
   Lost Horizon,
   The Vanishing, etc.
6. *Flowers in the Attic*
7. *Gigi*
8. *Meet Me in St. Louis*
9. *White Heat*

Matinee III

1. *Three Men and a Baby*
2. *The Facts of Life*
3. *Time after Time*
4. *Short Circuit*
5. *Separate Tables*
6. *Fiddler on the Roof*
7. *The Longest Day*
8. *All about Eve*
9. *Sea of Love*

Book Club

1. *The Little Minister*
   James M. Barrie
2. *The Turn of the Screw*
   Henry James
3. *The Last of the Mohicans*
   James Fenimore Cooper
4. *No Exit*
   Jean-Paul Sartre
5. *Catch-22*
   Joseph Heller
6. *An Unfinished Woman*
   Lillian Hellman
7. *Henry IV*
   William Shakespeare
8. *A Stranger in a Strange Land*
   Robert Heinlein
9. *Northwest Passage*
   Kenneth Roberts

Book Club II

1. *Go Tell It on the Mountain*
   James Baldwin
2. *The Thirty-nine Steps*
   John Buchan
3. *Oliver Twist*
   Charles Dickens
4. *Room at the Top*
   John Braine
5. *Lie Down in Darkness*
   William Styron
6. "A Season in Hell"
   Arthur Rimbaud
7. *Things Fall Apart*
   Chinua Achebe
8. *East of Eden*
   John Steinbeck
9. "Essay on Man"
   Alexander Pope

Book Club III

1. *Point Counter Point*
   Aldous Huxley
2. *The Lower Depths*
   Maxim Gorky
3. *Letters from the Underworld*
   Fyodor Dostoevski
4. *The 42nd Parallel*
   John Dos Passos
5. *Middlemarch*
   George Eliot
6. *Twelfth Night*
   William Shakespeare
7. *The Sun Also Rises*
   Ernest Hemingway
8. *Two Women*
   Alberto Moravia
9. *So Big*
   Edna Ferber

Book Club IV

1. *Seventeen*
   Booth Tarkington
2. *Ring Round the Moon*
   Jean Anouilh
3. *Man and Superman*
   George Bernard Shaw
4. *Washington Square*
   Henry James
5. *Much Ado about Nothing*
   William Shakespeare
6. *1984*
   George Orwell
7. *Pale Horse, Pale Rider*
   Katherine Anne Porter
8. *A Month in the Country*
   Ivan Turgenev
9. *Heart of Darkness*
   Joseph Conrad

Alphacryptics

1. nohow   2. fatback, finback   3. skip rope   4. joyless
5. bold-faced lie   6. box camera   7. checkpoint   8. no
smoking   9. round robin   10. smallpox

Alphacryptics II

1. stereotyped   2. day in, day out   3. behind times   4. little
woman   5. mixed blessing   6. light bulb   7. square dance
8. front porch   9. double duty   10. leftover

Word Meaning

Double Identities

1. Billy Crystal   2. Ginger Rogers   3. Gene Wilder   4. Spike
Lee   5. Tom Hanks   6. Pearl Buck   7. Mel Brooks   8. Mickey
Mantle

Double Identities II

1. Johnny Cash   2. Holly Hunter   3. Dean Martin   4. Joey
Bishop   5. Art Carney   6. Wilt Chamberlain   7. Kitty Kelly
8. Grace Slick   9. Fats Domino

Double Identities III

1. Ruby Dee   2. Sally Field   3. Peter Coyote   4. Merle
Haggard   5. Victor Mature   6. Tipper Gore   7. Saul Bellow
8. Benny Goodman   9. Beau Bridges

Equivokes
1. b   2. a   3. b   4. c   5. a   6. b   7. a
8. b   9. b   10. b   11. b   12. a   13. c

Equivokes II
1. a   2. c   3. a   4. c   5. b   6. a   7. b
8. a   9. b   10. a   11. c   12. a   13. b

Trivia Word Search

Ziggurat
1. zeitgeist   2. zwieback   3. zombie   4. zilch   5. zoysia
6. Zeppelin   7. Zurich   8. Ziegfeld   9. zero gravity
10. Zapata   11. zenith   12. zoom lens   13. zephyr
14. zucchini   15. zip code   16. zaftig   17. zinfandel   18. zoot
suit   19. Zen Buddhism   20. Zionism

Ziggurat

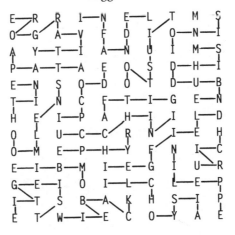

"Y" Knot
1. Yellowstone   2. "YMCA"   3. yellow fever   4. yarrow
5. Yalta   6. William Butler Yeats   7. Yorkshire pudding
8. Yom Kippur   9. "Yankee Doodle"   10. yin and yang
11. yoga   12. yogurt   13. yakitori   14. Yemen   15. Yonkers
16. yearling   17. Yuletide

"Y" Knot

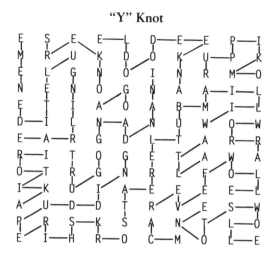

OD'd on "O"

1. Oregon Trail   2. Orpheus   3. Oscar   4. Oberon
5. Outback   6. orchid   7. Olympics   8. olfactory
9. Oedipus   10. Oxford   11. obsolescence   12. Ovid
13. Lee Harvey Oswald   14. Ozarks   15. osculate
16. Oceania   17. Oklahoma   18. Osiris

OD'd on "O"

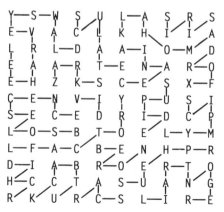

Valedictorian

1. veterinarian   2. vertebrate   3. Vivian   4. Vivaldi
5. vampire   6. vacuum   7. vacation   8. *Vanity Fair*
9. Verona   10. V-E Day   11. Voice of America   12. virtuoso
13. vice squad   14. viper   15. vagrant   16. Vatican
17. *Vertigo*   18. vespers   19. vicarious   20. vegetarian

Valedictorian

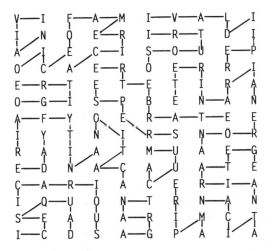

T Square

1. *Twelfth Night*   2. Trafalgar   3. Tasmanian   4. tempera
5. Tripoli   6. tumbrel   7. tempest   8. Teflon   9. teddy bear
10. *Tyrannosaurus*   11. tongue twister   12. Trojan War
13. Tiki   14. triennial   15. testosterone   16. theorem
17. tornado   18. Tierra del Fuego   19. Tory   20. Tonkin

T Square

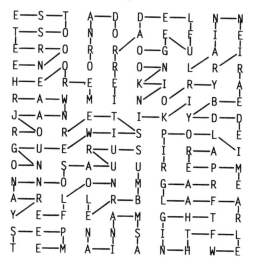

Relatively Speaking

My Cousin Charley

1. Dialogue and euphoria contain all the vowels: a, e, i, o and u.
2. Munster and Sternum are anagrams.
3. Moby Dick and Jane Eyre each have four letters.
4. Chinos, cello, and ghost contain letters in alphabetical order.
5. Cancan and bonbon contain doubled identical syllables.
6. Adieu and bureau can both be made into plurals with an "x."
7. Pout and gout, complain and pain, rhyme.

Charley's Cats

1. cathedral   2. catamaran   3. muscatels   4. scatology
5. decathlon   6. masticate   7. cataracts   8. medicated
9. suffocate   10. lubricate

Charley's Aunts

1. headhunter   2. orangutan   3. nocturnal   4. paramount
5. sauternes   6. raconteur   7. turntable   8. antifraud
9. flatulent   10. tarantula   11. debutante   12. abduction
13. astronaut   14. suntanned

Charley's Uncles
1. unicycle   2. antiulcer   3. corpulent   4. unbalanced
5. luckiness   6. masculine   7. lunchtime   8. ambulance
9. unethical   10. scoundrel   11. succulent   12. cruelness
13. affluence   14. counselor

Cousinly
1. suspicion   2. incurious   3. seclusion   4. neurotics
5. excursion   6. custodian   7. scouting   8. seduction
9. collusion   10. viscount   11. confusion   12. tenacious
13. carousing   14. inclusion   15. contentious

Aunt Amelia Visits the Zoo
1. zebra   2. wolf   3. hippos   4. otter   5. leopard
6. ocelots   7. raccoon   8. caiman   9. tortoise   10. coyote
Zoologist Level   11. taipan   12. siamangs

Aunt Amelia Visits the Dog Show
1. poodles   2. corgi   3. pointer   4. Irish terrier   5. spaniels
6. Saint Bernard   7. samoyed   8. basset hounds   9. English
setters   10. Labrador

Aunt Amelia Visits the Aviary
1. tern   2. egret   3. heron   4. magpies   5. condor
6. pigeon   7. warbler   8. pelican   9. woodhen   10. moorhen
Ornithologist Level   11. titmouse   12. grosbeak

Aunt Amelia Visits the Aquarium
1. clam   2. oyster   3. tuna   4. shark   5. bluegill   6. sardine
7. lobster   8. blowfish   9. flounder   10. stingray   11. barnacle
12. manatee   13. mussels

Aunt Amelia Visits the Botanic Garden
1. aster   2. daisy   3. sedum   4. salvia   5. lupine   6. crocus
7. petunia   8. oleander   9. geraniums   10. clematis
11. myrtle   **Green Thumb Level**   12. astilbe   13. freesia

Trivia

Lit*mus* Test
1. Uncle Remus   2. Albert Camus   3. Musetta   4. Musketeer
5. mussels   6. mustache   7. Momus   8. shamus   9. musical
10. mushroom   11. Muses   12. Nostradamus

Lit Test
1. lilliputian   2. Bunyanesque   3. Cinderella   4. Judas
5. bacchanal, bacchanalian, or bacchic   6. Tarzan   7. fagin
8. jeremiad   9. jezebel

Trivia Anagrams

What's in a Name?
1. Robert DeNiro
2. Sally Field
3. Adolf Hitler
4. Stevie Wonder
5. Gloria Steinem
6. Oprah Winfrey
7. Steve Martin
8. Clint Eastwood
9. Phil Donahue

What's in a Name II?
1. Norman Mailer
2. Edgar Allan Poe
3. Ernest Hemingway
4. Sir Arthur Conan Doyle
5. Emily Dickinson
6. Henry David Thoreau
7. Tennessee Williams
8. Agatha Christie
9. Edith Wharton

Global Power
1. Peru   2. Iran   3. Niger   4. Burma   5. Libya   6. Italy
7. Crete   8. Spain   9. Yemen   10. Israel   11. Persia
12. Angola   13. Algeria   14. Iceland   15. Palestine
Bonus   1. Bolivia   2. Brazil   3. Chad   4. Chile   5. Congo
6. Cyprus   7. Guinea   8. Holland   9. Japan   10. Jordan
11. Kashmir   12. Morocco   13. Panama   14. Turkey
15. Wales   16. Zaire

Global Power II
1. Las Vegas, Nevada, U.S.A.
2. Darwin, Australia
3. Tunis, Tunisia
4. Venice, Italy
5. Lagos, Nigeria
6. Detroit, Michigan, U.S.A.
7. Athens, Greece
8. Valencia, Spain, or Valencia, Venezuela
9. Seoul, South Korea
10. Leeds, England
11. San Diego, California, U.S.A.
12. Nassau, Bahamas
13. Tucson, Arizona, U.S.A.
14. Caracas, Venezuela
15. Los Angeles, California, U.S.A.

Global Power III
1. madras (Madras, India)
2. bath, also baht (Bath, England)
3. toledo, also looted, tooled (Toledo, Ohio, U.S.A.; Toledo, Spain)
4. buffalo (Buffalo, New York, U.S.A.)
5. paris, also pairs (Paris, France)
6. warsaw (Warsaw, Poland)
7. providence (Providence, Rhode Island, U.S.A.)
8. phoenix (Phoenix, Arizona, U.S.A.)
9. manila, also animal, lamina (Manila, Philippines)
10. hamburg (Hamburg, Germany)
11. bordeaux (Bordeaux, France)
12. victoria (Victoria, Hong Kong; Victoria, British Columbia, Canada)

Anagrams

Symbolically Speaking
1. period, provide
2. colon, colony
3. plus, pulse
4. asterisk, mistakers
5. bracket, backrest
6. plus, slurp
7. colon, uncool
8. comma, hammock
9. bracket, backbiter
10. colon, volcano
11. plus, juleps

Want Adz from A to Z
1. knifed   2. gremlin   3. yogurt   4. wagered   5. varlet
6. esthete   7. misdeed   8. liberal   9. battle   10. xis
11. outspend   12. zoned   13. penalty   14. rampant
15. smokier   16. dimple   17. armrest   18. unnamed
19. nodule   20. fitness   21. hepcats   22. tragedy
23. coupons   24. jitter   25. intones   26. querier

Want Adz II, Short List
1. flatiron   2. misspelt   3. organist   4. boneless   5. virginal
6. crumpets   7. avarice   8. untimely   9. truelove
10. regiment   11. quartile   12. dominoes   13. euphoric
14. gardenia   15. sidestep   16. parried   17. heretics
18. wormiest   19. insisted   20. littered   21. yatter   22. niceness

Want Adz III, Short List
1. murderer   2 aerosol   3. bogeyman   4. coutures
5. vitamins   6. quartets   7. poloist   8. opposer   9. nepotism
10. weirdoes   11. yardmen   12. garnish   13. depletes
14. ultimate   15. infringe   16. trendier   17. lopsided
18. emotions   19. happiest   20. refunded   21. fiendish
22. sunlight

Dog Catcher
1. girlhood   2. devouring   3. knowledge   4. groundhog
5. downgrade   6. wrongdoer   7. dragonfly   8. exploding
9. vagabond   10. shadowing   11. goldenrod   12. congested
13. radiology   14. bandwagon   15. mortgaged   16. obligated
17. guidebook   18. undergone   19. orangeade   20. hydrogen
21. headlong   22. marigold   23. diagnosis   24. prodigies

Manhunt
1. abdominal   2. imaginary   3. macaroni   4. lamebrain
5. malignant   6. dynamite   7. impatient   8. flamingo
9. important   10. gramophone   11. spearmint   12. emotional
13. benchmark   14. abnormal   15. sacrament   16. cinematic
17. dominance   18. geranium   19. machinery   20. rainstorm
21. menopause   22. magnetic   23. comedian   24. enumerate

Category Puzzles

Joint Custody
1. window   2. house   3. sand   4. money   5. square   6. bush or Bush   7. pipe   8. buster or Buster   9. fool's   10. blind

Joint Custody II
1. bull   2. cat   3. dog   4. bug   5. birth   6. cut
7. four or 4-   8. fox   9. ice   10. Northern or northern

Joint Custody III
1. shell   2. spring   3. pig or Pig   4. love   5. hope or Hope
6. glass or Glass   7. electric   8. potato   9. United   10. smoking

Joint Custody IV
1. thumb   2. frost or Frost   3. Western or western   4. flying
5. ginger   6. English   7. spoon   8. counter   9. French or french   10. time or Time

Joint Custody V
1. horse   2. face   3. second   4. show   5. inner   6. Turkish
7. bat   8. Court or court   9. free   10. kid or Kid

Common Denominator
Things That Are Green: grass, money, Kermit
Woody Allen Movies: Bananas, Manhattan, Sleeper
Brushes: paint, tooth, toilet bowl
Islands: Canary, Society, Virgin
Cakes: cheese, coffee, wedding

Common Denominator II
Moores: Demi, Dudley, Mary Tyler
Martins: Dean, Mary, Steve
Woodys: Allen, Guthrie, Woodpecker
Barrymores: Drew, Ethel, Lionel
Stars Who Use One Name: Cher, Madonna, and Prince

Common Denominator III
Stones: Rolling, gall, Flint or flint
Root Plants: ginger, peanuts, sarsaparilla
1960s Dances: pony, jerk, mashed potato
Poets: Frost, Burns, Browning
Things Found in a Car Trunk: dead body, jack, flare

Common Denominator IV
"Yellow＿＿＿＿: sunflower, coward, fever
Famous Beaches: Miami, Omaha, Ipanema
Women's Names in Beatles Song Titles: Julia, Rita, Michelle
Things You Pick: cotton, guitar, nose
Things You Catch: cold, train, fish

Common Denominator V
Brontë Sisters: Emily, Anne, Charlotte
Apostles: John, Thomas, Simon
Steaks: chuck, round, flank
Famous Blind People: Oedipus Rex, Ray Charles, Helen Keller
Famous George/Georges: Balanchine, Harrison, Pompidou

Common Denominator VI
Things That Go Up: elevator, blood pressure, zipper
Types of Licenses: marriage, dog, poetic
Things You Blow: kiss, nose, bubble
Types of Mail: junk, air, registered
Grands: Canyon, piano, slam

Letter Patterns

Angelic Devilry
1. jangle   2. general   3. lovebird   4. glance   5. dissolve
6. divulged   7. lasagne   8. vandalize   9. avoidable
10. halogen   11. levied, veiled   12. gasoline   13. drivel
14. lineage   15. evildoer   16. finagled   17. genial   18. gnarliest

Guys & Gals
1. guilty 2. flagpole 3. bodyguard 4. tangelo 5. singular
6. burgundy 7. synagogue 8. young 9. hangnail
10. laughter 11. gauzy 12. sugary 13. yogurt 14. ladybug
15. elegant 16. neurology 17. hooligan 18. gurney

Twofers

Award Night 1. awkwardly 2. hungriest 3. lengthier
4. whistling 5. boardwalk 6. hindsight 7. washboard
8. arrowhead 9. afterward 10. gunfight **Challenge:** Clio

Coca-Cola 1. alcoholic 2. bachelor 3. illogical 4. stockcar
5. cockroach 6. washcloth 7. democracy 8. scorecard
9. crosswalk 10. coatrack **Challenge:** nut and leaf

Moby Dick 1. tomboy 2. backside 3. duckling 4. homebody
5. handpick 6. hymnbook 7. sidekick 8. bickered
9. symbolic 10. wickedly **Challenge:** "Call me Ishmael."

Santa Claus 1. stanza 2. against 3. musical 4. analyst
5. casual 6. nostalgia 7. upscale 8. masculine 9. pheasant
10. stagehand **Challenge:** Australia

Talk Show 1. cocktail 2. seaworthy 3. blanketed
4. honeydews 5. wishbone 6. teakettle 7. wholesale
8. township 9. walkathon 10. folktale
Challenge: movie-making

Babe Ruth 1. author 2. thrust 3. abbey 4. haircut 5. barbell
6. butcher 7. bareback 8. crutch 9. fourth 10. beanbag
Challenge: John Goodman

Hot Dog 1. both 2. gourd 3. thou 4. historic 5. photo
6. indigo 7. gumdrop 8. chocolate 9. pagoda 10. hereto
Challenge: performing in a showy manner, especially in surfing
or skiing

Round Table 1. greyhound 2. alphabet 3. adjourned
4. introduce 5. nourished 6. dangerous 7. veritable
8. celebrate 9. meatball 10. scoundrel
Challenge: Algonquin Hotel

Crew Neck 1. wreck 2. kitchen 3. microwave 4. escrow
5. henpeck 6. reckon 7. nickname 8. cartwheel 9. curfew
10. cowrite   **Challenge:** Lana Turner

Mom, Dad 1. ammo 2. modem 3. mambo 4. comma
5. decade 6. aided 7. daffodil 8. commando 9. symptom
10. dandelion   **Challenge:** entraps, pastern, arpents, trepans

Soul Mate 1. hilarious 2. carousel 3. hourglass 4. doldrums
5. basement 6. demitasse 7. nightmare 8. muskmelon
9. ghoulish 10. barometer   **Challenge:** Galatea

Onion Field 1. flickered 2. moonshine 3. opinionated
4. lifeguard 5. frolicked 6. communion 7. qualified
8. continuous 9. nontoxic 10. companion
Challenge: Joseph Wambaugh

Zig, Zag 1. gizmo 2. oozing 3. magazine 4. gazebo 5. glitz
6. organza 7. stargazer 8. zoologist 9. gazelle 10. cognizant
Challenge: 1846

Army, Navy 1. armory 2. military 3. varying 4. majority
5. anchovy 6. anymore 7. smarty 8. voluntary 9. pharmacy
10. vineyard   **Challenge:** Annapolis, Maryland, and West Point,
New York, respectively

Milan, Italy 1. alumni 2. litany 3. laxity 4. mainly
5. typical 6. animal 7. labyrinth 8. monorail 9. policeman
10. daylight   **Challenge:** Milano

Far Out 1. dwarf 2. utopia 3. tofu 4. fabric 5. doubt
6. burrito 7. starfish 8. mousetrap 9. earful 10. tugboat
Challenge: Allen Ginsberg

Shin Bone 1. sandwich 2. sixteenth 3. debonair 4. abdomen
5. rebellion 6. homebound 7. christen 8. workbench
9. cushioned 10. hypnotist   **Challenge:** tibia

Fish Soup 1. flourish 2. homespun 3. sculptor 4. firehouse
5. autopsy 6. shoplift 7. firsthand 8. courtship 9. spacious
10. poisonous   **Challenge:** bouillabaisse

Toy Box 1. attorney 2. geometry 3. oxblood 4. typhoon
5. lavatory 6. bodysuit 7. exhibitor 8. matrimony
9. textbook 10. obnoxious   **Challenge:** skates, board games,
marbles

Fast Food 1. wasteful 2. faintest 3. firewood 4. masterful
5. fantasize 6. proofed 7. beefsteak 8. comforted
9. confounder 10. floodgate   **Challenge:** golden arches
(McDonald's symbol)

• Index •

Answer pages are in italics.